This book is dedicated to the very special people who
made such a difference to my young life, my social
workers Jeff, Ann, Jimmy, John and David.

CONTENTS

INTRODUCTION

Not long ago I started working for a homeless shelter founded by a friend of mine. It was in a church and I arrived one evening to find a nineteen-year-old girl waiting for me.

'I can't go home, can you help me?'

'Have you tried the police?'

'They sent me here.'

'What happened?'

'Some girls. They're gonna mess me up, serious.'

I called the police.

'She refused to go home,' an officer said. 'There's nothing we can do. We kept her in a cell for a bit, but our hands are tied unless there's a crime.'

I went back to the girl, whose name was Chloe. She had recently dyed her hair black, which may have been an attempt at disguise. She had a few small tattoos on her arms, and was nursing a cup of tea with shaking hands.

She reminded me of me.

I used to roam the streets at night after running from the

children's home, looking for I-don't-know-what and ending up in Trafalgar Square. As Chloe talked, it was clear she was involved with some seriously nasty people – male and female. I could understand why she didn't want to be out on the streets at night.

The other thing I noticed was that Chloe was angry. Her muscles were taut and she looked as though she could explode at any moment. I knew that Chloe was using that anger to hide her fear – and that her aggressive approach to life perhaps came from the lack of love she'd received as child.

Displays of anger in young people are one of the key reasons they don't get the help they need. I had to go into hospital a few years ago and, when I saw my medical files on the table next to my bed, I picked them up and started reading. Apart from the many entries by midwives who'd written about me when I was pregnant, expressing concern and stating that, as I'd been in care and hadn't been in contact with any doctor or hospital, I was 'at risk', I was completely bowled over by the entries from when I gave birth. The files said I was aggressive and hostile – and violent! In reality, I was so scared, so alone, and I was just reaching out to the nurses for help. I was probably a bit out of it because of the drugs they'd given me, but they'd made completely the wrong assumptions about me.

All too often, anger and fear go hand-in-hand.

Chloe had been part of a gang but something had made them turn against her. I didn't ask what it was, I didn't want to know; but she indicated that there had been a lot of 'sleeping around' with different boyfriends. She was beside herself. No teenager deserves to feel that kind of fear. We made her a bed in our section of the church, so she'd sleep with us. Chloe was so grateful and kept thanking us over and over.

The next morning was Saturday and Chloe wouldn't leave the church. I called a contact at the local council to see if there was something they could do, but they were against us and, in so many words, said not to come knocking at their door, even though they knew the people she was scared of – and understood that she was right to be scared of them.

At last, we found a place of safety a long way out of the area, in a B&B. The local council for that area took our concerns seriously and they managed to get her housed.

As I left Chloe in the B&B, knowing she had a shot at a new start in a new town, I thought of the many dangers she was likely to face as a vulnerable, lonely young girl in need of love and support – from sexual predators to drug and alcohol addiction. The odds were stacked against her, like they had been for me, for all of the people in this book.

In my first book, *Hackney Child*, published in 2014, I told the story of how, as a nine-year-old child of alcoholic parents, I had walked into a police station with my brothers and asked to be taken into care. The follow-up, *Tainted Love*, told the stories of some of the kids whom I lived with in children's homes.

Although I had a difficult time in care, care didn't damage me, I was damaged by the time I ran to find help – by lack of love. I never had a cuddle from my parents, who were frozen in terms of physical contact (I never even saw them cuddle each other). The harm that the lack of love can do to a child is far greater than most people imagine. *Neglected* tells my story and the stories of others I have met through my outreach work, of our search for love, as children and as adults.

We have shared our stories because we want more than anything to stop anyone else from having to endure what we did, as well as help those who are suffering to understand their behaviour and know that there is help out there. And to know, no matter how bad things are, there is always hope. And with hope, there is the possibility to heal and to build an entirely new and better kind of life.

That these courageous people, who are still fighting daily battles with addictions and their pasts, are able to tell their stories at all is thanks to the care workers who brought them back to an understanding of what love really means. While Parts One and Two tell the stories of people who, like myself, suffered from a lack of love, Part Three – *The Other Side of Love* – contains incredible stories told from the perspective of those unsung heroes, the care workers who fight every day to save and rebuild lives, the adopters, foster carers and social workers who go to extraordinary lengths to help the children in their care.

So many children have suffered for lack of love and have fought in different ways to replace that love as they became adults. They found artificial feelings of love in drugs, in alcohol, or through sex – they used them as a way to 'feel' love, and to feel as though they were wanted and that it was possible for them to be loved. The results are often disastrous – with huge costs to themselves, the people around them (in some cases their children) and to society.

Their shocking stories make for tough reading but,

remember, they have come through their experiences and have changed – with help. It's only through learning about the circumstances that drove them into these extraordinary states of mind that we can hope to understand and help them.

We should never forget that these people were once children who needed help and didn't get it. And, as adults, they need our help more than ever.

When we encounter a girl like Chloe then we must think twice and see past the angry 'problem child' to the scared and lost little girl underneath, and we must do something positive to give her hope, before it's too late.

Part One:

THE WRONG SIDE OF LOVE

HOPE

A cold room, light streaming in with the draught through un-curtained windows. Mattress on the hard floor; we're surrounded on all sides by clothes, bags and my suitcase. This is so Lauren can't climb out and crawl around the room in the morning. She'll die if she eats the mould growing on the walls.

The only 'furniture' (apart from the mattress), is the large beanbag in the lounge.

The leaves are turning gold on the poorly-looking trees on the narrow street lined with cars, parked bumper to bumper. There is condensation on the windows, sparkling in the sunlight, but I don't dare put the boiler on for hot water or heating because it floods the communal stairs and the flat below. I've picked the mushrooms that were growing in the gloom of the stairwell so that Lauren or some other child won't die from eating or touching them.

No one knows I'm here. Everyone thinks I'm coping. Social services are one step behind me.

It's 1994. I'm twenty years old and have been on the run with my baby for two years now.

I ran from the care system I needed so badly, from my abusive foster family, from Mum and Dad – my past, my life, my pain, my fear, so out of my control.

Two years earlier, I was dumped out of the care system because I turned eighteen. I made all the right sounds and did all the right things. I proved that I was bright and showed promise. I showed how the system could work well. I wanted to study law, to become a solicitor so I could help people like me.

I was also an emotional wreck and no one was close enough to me to know.

I'd hung on with my foster family placement, which is where I had been since I was seventeen.

Review of Placement Agreement 9th January 1991
Over-all aim of placement: For Hope to finish her education.
Relationship with foster family: Satisfactory relationships generally – very close with Pat. Very active family . . . Two other foster teenagers, and two teenagers and two little ones 'home grown' and one or two child-minded. Hope has her own room and enjoys having privacy into which to withdraw and study.

Yeah, right. No mention in that report of the nightmare of that family. My room was somewhere to hide. The two other teenagers she fostered for money. She never showed the social worker the part of the house where we had to live – separate from her family, in bare, unheated rooms. Our fridge was filled with her scraps – old meat and veg she would have otherwise thrown – and she baked it into inedible pies, while her family's fridge had a lock on it. She put us to work babysitting and later used me to sort out her accounting – telling me to hide money off their books so the tax man wouldn't find out. I couldn't say anything. Otherwise they'd stick me in a hostel. At least at my foster home I'd been able to do part-time jobs, have a bed and roof.

Just keep it together, get through my exams, get a place at college – that had been my mantra. I kept everything to myself. I'm good at that. When Sharon, the social worker, came to visit (she was a trainee and not much older than me – but she was a lady I came to love dearly), my foster mum kept the doors to our section of the house closed.

My foster mum hid things, and so did I, but I think Sharon had a feeling something was wrong; that there was something I wasn't telling her.

I survived, though, and then, a few weeks before I turned eighteen, I told Sharon what the foster family was really like. I showed her everything.

Sharon believed me.

An investigation took place.

But I was left homeless.

'I have nowhere to stay,' I told social services. 'What am I supposed to do tonight?'

'Stay at a friend's house,' was their advice.

If I'd been missing a few weeks earlier it would have been a big thing but now I was about to turn eighteen, it wasn't. I refused point-blank. They had to do something. Legally, they had to, until I was eighteen, so they said I could live with some other foster carers, but only until my birthday.

I wasn't ready.

They said I could still receive funding for college to study law and that if I found a private flat, I could receive housing benefit.

I couldn't.

The pain and fear were there together, ever present. I couldn't be on my own, not yet, I wasn't ready. I couldn't go from being in care to nothing, from one day to the next.

No one loves me. I've no one to love. They just want to get me out, so I'm not their burden any more.

I found a flat a few days after my eighteenth birthday. A few weeks after that I had a meeting with Sharon about funding for my college placement.

'I'm not going to college,' I told her. 'I'm pregnant.'

'Then there is no more we can do for you but discharge you from care as of this moment.'

They were the words I was expecting. If I couldn't be in care, then I'd make my own family.

They asked me what my plans were. They said I could have a hostel place but I would have to come back to Hackney.

No way.

'I'm going to get married,' I said.

So they paid the deposit on my studio flat and I was signed out of care.

If I was going to keep my baby – which is what I wanted, desperately – then I thought I needed to say I was getting married. Single mums my age who'd been in care and who got pregnant had their babies removed.

Such a surgical term. 'Your baby will be removed.' Like

they're taking out your appendix – more like ripping out your heart.

Another thing I had to do to keep my baby – and to survive – was to keep all of my problems and worries bottled up. By saying I was getting married I thought I'd come across as respectable in the eyes of social services.

The next stage of my plan was to disappear. This wasn't as hard as I thought. Social services offered no advice about being pregnant or being a mum. I didn't register for antenatal. On the four occasions a letter from the midwife fell through the letterbox, I moved home. They couldn't keep up.

I had no scans, no idea what I should be doing while I was pregnant. I just let time pass. I was scared, in emotional pain, and worrying about what would happen, whether they would take my baby. I wasn't drinking, wasn't taking drugs, I was just surviving each day, sure as one follows the next.

When I was eight months along, I got sick and had to go to the doctor. He commented that he wasn't expecting me to be pregnant, let alone eight months pregnant.

He reached for pen and paper, asking me who I was seeing with regard to my pregnancy.

'No one.'

He stopped, pen hanging over paper.

'You haven't seen anyone since you became pregnant? No health professional?'

I shook my head.

I jerk awake. It's night-time, I'm in a hospital bed and terri-fied. And the pain. Oh my God. What is that?

Figures are around me, the room is dark, then flickers into light, sharp strip lights. I blink through a haze of tears and cry again as the wave of pain tears through my body. I reach out desperately, begging for help, and grab hold of someone. Why is there so much pain?

'Stop that!' a nurse shouts, pulling my hands away.

'Someone please help me, I don't understand what's going on.'

'Calm down! You're having a baby; everything's fine.'

'But it hurts!'

'It's supposed to, now shut up!'

I pull myself up, so I am half-sitting, half-leaning over the side of the bed.

'I – I haven't been to antenatal. I don't know . . . Don't know what to expect.'

One of the nurses pushes me back on to the bed.

'We'll give you something for the pain, but just shut up and lie still!'

My baby's coming. I don't know what to do.

'What do I do?'

'When you feel the pain, that's a contraction.'

'What's that? I don't understand.'

'When you feel the contraction, just push.'

'Push, push what? What should I push?'

I collapse back on the bed as another wave passes over me. Something must be wrong. Surely it wasn't supposed to be like this.

But I don't know, I don't know, I don't know, I keep saying until, somewhere in the red darkness behind my eyes pressed shut, something breaks, tears and explodes from within me.

So scared I can't breathe. I am holding my breath and I don't know whether I need to breathe in or out. Finally I gasp and open my eyes to see a baby being lifted out of me.

The nurses look concerned, the baby comes up and up. A girl.

'Is she supposed to be like that? Why is she so blue?'

'The umbilical cord is wrapped around her neck,' one of the nurses says, leaving the room with my little baby.

'Where is she taking my baby?'

'You've torn quite badly; we're going to have to stitch you up.'

I can't move, my legs are in stirrups. I start to shout and scream for my baby.

'If you don't stop, we'll leave you where you are and you won't be stitched up.'

I lie back, look at the ceiling, trying to smother my whimpers, so they will sew me up and let me see my baby. It takes them a lifetime to finish.

'Right,' the horrible nurse in charge says; 'you can see her now.'

And they bring her in and a nurse lies her on my chest.

'But I don't know what to do. How to hold her, nothing.'

'Just feed her!' the nurse yells. 'It's not hard.'

'I can't, I don't know how. I'm so sorry; I didn't go to antenatal care.'

The nurse looks me in the eye for a moment, shakes her head in disgust and walks out. The rest of the nurses follow, leaving me with my baby, not knowing what to do. One of them reappears with a bottle a few minutes later.

'Don't bother trying to breastfeed her. You better use this,' and she leaves.

Now I have my baby, I feel even more alone than ever.

All I ever wanted was for someone to hold my hand and tell me that they loved me.

I had my baby girl and I was grateful for that. But at the same time my little glass bubble I'd put us in was starting to crack. I was so alone. I had no one to help me. I wouldn't open the door when the health visitor came around and frequently got myself into a panic with baby Lauren. It was just so overwhelming.

She couldn't keep her milk down. I was panicking. I took her to the hospital and they said, 'We are keeping you in.'

I didn't ask questions. This was serious.

But it wasn't, not in the sense I imagined.

I was using the wrong-sized teat on the bottle. There were different sizes. I'd just used the one that came with the bottle.

They kept us in for four days before discharging us. They wanted to see what I was like with Lauren.

And I was fine.

But inside, I was a wreck. I didn't know that there was such a thing as post-natal depression. My mind, already so stressed, was filled with awful thoughts, the worst one of which was that social services were after my baby. I played out multiple scenarios where I would have to escape from social services, who in reality were barely aware of my existence. I moved and moved again until no one knew where I was, and I was in a town where I'd never even been before in a flat with mushrooms growing on the stairs, no heating and it was getting colder and colder each morning, until I could see my breath condense in the bedroom and frost on the inside of the glass.

I'd never felt so alone, so scared.

JOHNNY/JEMMA

Like all the people whose stories are in this book, I met Jemma (formerly Johnny) through my outreach work. We ran into one another when I was going through a tough time, mentally. The first thing that struck me about Jemma was her looks. She was stunningly beautiful and only her eyes hinted at her long and difficult journey. Before long, she was sharing her story with me and, by doing so, Jemma helped me more than perhaps she knows. Jemma's story makes it clear that if we face our fears and follow our hearts, we can accomplish almost anything.

I already knew I was a girl by the time my mum, drunk, was having sex behind the sofa to supplement her income while I sat watching the TV, sound turned up (*Go, Go, Power Rangers!*) to try and cover the human noises coming from behind me on the carpet. These were my earliest memories.

I must have given the obstetrician pause for thought when I was born but, still, despite my 'ambiguous genitalia' he declared me a boy, just like that. By the time I was three I knew he'd made a mistake, along with everyone else. I played like a girl – just couldn't play any other way, though I would have to hide my games from Dad because he'd beat his little boy, a futile and bullying attempt to make a man of his son. I was too slow to hide the My Little Pony one day when Dad came up behind me, yelling, 'You fucking gay bastard!' and then the world exploded into millions of shining coloured stars before I could turn around. My ears hummed for hours afterwards, I winced as Mum tried to comb my hair. He hit her, too, and my older brother and sister, but never as much as he hit me.

When the beatings didn't work, I had an operation. The doctor told Mum and Dad not to tell anyone: 'Our secret,' Mum told me, through tears. I felt then, as a six-year-old, that Mum knew this was wrong but us girls were power-less to do anything about it. Dad and the doctor wanted me to be a man and that was that, end of discussion.

The reassignment surgery, carried out on the NHS, was, I now think, the cheapest one they could do – moving muscle and tissue around without worrying about the long-term consequences for me, worrying what it would be like to live with what they'd done, what it would feel like. 'Feelings' were not high on their list of priorities. I was an embarrassment to humanity, and felt barely human as I listened to the surgeon deciding and then talking through what he was going to do, without looking at me, apart from a brief hello and goodbye. I knew they were wrong, wrong, wrong, but I decided to believe him when he promised he could turn me into a little boy and, as Mum and Dad wanted this, and I wanted them to love me, to be a proper child to a dad who wouldn't beat me and might even like me, I went ahead and watched the patterns of paint on the white ceiling spiral above me when they gave me the lovely premeds, and it was time to count down: ten, nine, eight . . .

Waking up dry-mouthed, in pain, with bandages that pulled my skin tight, it didn't feel right. As soon as I had the strength, I lifted the sheets and looked. My stomach was yellow with antiseptic from the belly button down and bandages covered everything. Being in hospital was hard, sleepless nights from other sick children I didn't particularly feel like talking to; food that was too hard to eat even when I finally got my appetite back and was starving; and sleepless nights as the nurses clacked and clattered, rattling pills.

Funny thing was, I didn't feel any different. I still wanted to be a girl. Maybe with time, I thought.

I loved learning and was a bright child, keen to know everything the teachers wanted to tell me and more, but I ruined everything when, happy to show one and all I was now a boy, I showed my curious classmates the results of the operation. My form teacher, Miss Masters, took me to one side.

'Johnny, you're not supposed to show your peepee to anyone at school,' she said as kindly and clearly as possible.

'But, Miss, I've had an operation to become a proper boy. I want everyone to know so that they can be friends with me now.'

Although I loved lessons, I was lacking friends. Boys didn't want to play with me because I wasn't like them and didn't like football and fighting, and girls wouldn't play with me because I was, supposedly, a boy.

While most boys hid porn magazines from their mums and dads, I hid *Bella* and *Woman's Realm* under my mattress and it was there that, aged eleven, I learned about what it meant to be gay and lesbian and that some people had sex changes. One man, living as a woman, said he was transgender and, forever grateful to these wonderful magazines for all their knowledge and exploration of other worlds, I realised I wasn't alone. I looked the word up in a huge dictionary in the school library. So my gender identity didn't match my assigned sex. So, I thought, the operation hadn't worked and, therefore, to exist successfully in this world, to live and love, the closest I could get to what I felt was gay.

Mum, who was a lot more macho than most mums, and old school besides, knew this. I knew she loved me despite the fact I wasn't 'my father's son' because every now and then she'd quietly present me with a new My Little Pony that we both had to keep secret from Dad. When I was twelve she let me watch a TV documentary about a transgender woman called Julia. The outside world vanished as I watched, absorbed beyond distraction, fascinated. Mum and me wouldn't talk about my desires and I knew this was just how it had to be, but I understood what Mum was doing.

I also knew not to talk about my uncle, who was part of a religious cult, how he liked to get into bed with me and rub himself up against me and commit what his cult would call 'gross unnatural conduct' when Mum and Dad were out and he was babysitting. I hoped he'd go to hell.

My brother and sister knew but were just relieved it wasn't them that Uncle David picked on. It was my bad luck that I was a particularly beautiful dark-haired and feminine-looking little boy – a 'little angel', as Uncle David would say.

We lived in a three-bedroom house. Dad worked in a fire-extinguisher factory as some kind of foreman and we were well off compared to some families at school, but I would have swapped with the poorest. Dad held back most of his wages from Mum, giving her barely enough to live, let alone feed and clothe us. Most days, after tea, Dad would hit Mum who was ten years younger and almost half the size. Some nights were worse than others but this routine stayed the same until Mum started to drink before Dad got home, which made her clumsy and forgetful, and Dad, grateful for any excuse to yell, called her a stupid whore, a useless cow, and hit her even more. Running from the rages, I listened from my room as Dad blamed Mum for me, that 'little fucking poofter' and then I would hear through the wall as Dad, perhaps moved by Mum's sobs, or more likely the need for a good night's sleep, told her not to cry, that he was sorry, but if she would just try and be a better wife then he wouldn't have to hit her quite so much.

Because Mum started to drink through the day and she started having sex with strangers to pay for her growing addiction, she didn't notice that I started to eat more and more, stealing biscuits from the tin, bread from the barrel, sugar from the bowl, cereal from the box and this, along with seconds at school, as well as all the extras from the kids who didn't want the sandwiches their parents made for them, meant I started putting on lots of weight – and, by thirteen, Dad was calling me a *'fat* poofter'.

Dad kicked Mum out when I was eleven years old and said he was keeping us. We all wanted to go with Mum. Dad's new girlfriend was even younger than Mum. She wanted babies but needed to take special drugs to help her. I found the pills and threw them down the toilet, no more babies born to that monster.

The next morning I woke up in pain, Dad was pulling my hair, pulling, pulling, lifting me off the bed, yelling: 'You fucking little gay bastard!'

'Stop, Dad, please, stop!'

He let go, throwing me back down on the bed and then shouted as he grabbed the wardrobe and pulled and half-picked it up before throwing it on top of me. The terror of death that came at that moment was all-consuming. The mattress took some of the impact otherwise Dad would have been up for murder, or more likely convincing the police that I'd fallen from the wardrobe while trying to climb it, playing in my room. Next thing, the wardrobe was gone, Dad's arms were thicker than most men's, enlarged by lugging fire extinguishers around year after year; he was proud of those arms. It was impossible even to think about the possibility of resisting as pulled me up and started to smack my head on the dressing table, over and over until the stars danced in front of my crossed eyes, the words 'gay bastard' shouted, repeated over and over, coming through muffled to my singing ears. He stopped, but pulled my hair again, and dragged me, screaming, through the house, down the stairs, along the hall to the basement door, knees and hands thudding as I reached to hold my hair, to stop it being pulled, and then down to the ground to try and stop my body bouncing off the wooden stairs. He dropped me on a rug already unfurled on the cold concrete basement floor and quickly rolled me up inside, until I couldn't move. I had asthma and could hardly breathe as he sat on my chest, leaning in very close to say: 'I'm not done with you yet, you gay bastard. I'm going to come back and break every bone in your body. In fact, I might as well kill you, you're only going to die of AIDS anyway.' Then the pressure lifted and I heard his steps receding upwards; the door slammed and was locked.

I had to escape. He was going to kill me this time. I choked for lack of air and dust that seemed to leap from the rug every time I struggled to move. My arms were trapped behind me. I twisted and turned, starting to panic. The rug was so heavy and wound so tightly. I started to feel light-headed; I hadn't long before unconsciousness would grip me. Grabbing a breath of air, I twisted and practically dislocated an arm to pull it out from behind me, up and over my head and out of the top of the roll, and this gave me just enough space to start to squirm my way out. I lay panting on the cold floor for a good few minutes, until the pounding in my ears had faded to a soft hum.

The windows, ceiling height on the inside but at ground level on the outside, were really narrow. I was really fat. I had to try. Using metal shelves for a ladder, I clambered up. The inside of the pane was wet and, being February, freezing cold. The window latch, stiff from disuse, was slippery with water and didn't want to budge. I pulled and twisted at the lever until I was sweating, veins popping and, as I was about to give up, the lever squeaked. I pushed and the window opened upwards and outwards. Still dubious as to whether I'd fit, I was nevertheless the most highly motivated I'd ever been in my life, and so I reached through with both arms ahead and, pulling on the corner of a raised paving slab in the front garden, I hauled my head and shoulders through, and got as far as my hips before I got stuck, rain pelting on me as I wiggled, terrified that Dad would see me at any moment and would either drag me or kick me back down into that basement. Tearing my pyjamas, I strained, the metal frame bruising and cutting into my skin, the window now moving in its small iron frame as I pulled myself, millimetre by millimetre, into the outside world. Clutching my torn pyjama trousers, I didn't even feel the rain as I ran, crying, panting, head ringing, barefoot through the streets, running, running, running, in absolute fear of my life, until my breath gave out and, still fearful of being caught by Dad, I hid under a bush and, whether from shock or the cold, I passed out.

I woke up in a police station. Warm and dry and in someone else's clothes. It was 3a.m. I had no memory of getting here. The cops were kind and smiled at me, tight-lipped, but some of them didn't look me in the eye. I had a black eye and a shining lump in the middle of my forehead from where the wardrobe had hit me. I don't know whether they went to see my dad, they just told me that I was going to stay somewhere safe.

'Somewhere safe' turned out to be – thanks to a lack of care home places – a secure unit for deeply troubled children. Sure enough, it looked like a prison for kids, barbed wire curling over the tops of the walls, not a smile shared between the drab-looking staff. This was a jail for car thieves and drug addicts, most between fifteen and seventeen years old. I was by now thirteen, camp, feminine, quiet, broken, intelligent and liked to study. I might as well have had a target stuck on me.

'I'm going to die,' I thought as I was escorted into a room with four older boys who could immediately see what I was. Kids like to single out those who are different and had no trouble identifying me, for I was extraordinary in the worst possible way.

The next day in the bathroom, showering, I washed my hair before realising something wasn't right, the shampoo was too thin, the smell – I screamed. Someone had peed in my shampoo bottle. Darren, a tall, dark-haired, tanned boy, was top-boy and regularly trashed my things, shoved and pushed me, calling me a poof, at which point the others would join in. They even took the trouble to take it in turns to wake me up at different times through the night so I was zombie-tired the next day.

On the plus side, we drank milk, had chocolate and I could have a bath – things forbidden to me at home by Dad. We had to share the chores and I was quite happy behind the hoover or wielding a duster but, eventually, the abuse got to the point where I, the victim, was pulled aside for causing disruption among the other children.

'We didn't have this trouble before you got here,' one warden said as he walked me to a huge boardroom full of adults, where the leader of the local social services department, a terrifying lady called Irene, who walked with a limp (it was rumoured that she had a false leg and would beat kids with it), made me stand up in front of the other adults before saying: 'You are homosexual.'

The adults around the table seemed to loom darkly, in and out of focus as I watched the scene. It seemed to happen at a great distance. Light-headed, I looked down at my feet.

'Jonathan!' she snapped. 'You are homosexual, aren't you?'

I nodded.

'I can't hear you. I want you to tell us you are a homosexual. In your own words.'

I nodded and murmured a tiny 'Yeah' in reply.

'You are a threat to the other children, to the smooth running of this institution,' she said. 'It is necessary to isolate you.'

I was taken from the boy's side. 'Oh what relief!' I thought. 'Put the gay boy in with the girls. Of course, what could be better!'

But we stopped midway between the boys' and girls' dormitories. 'What's this?' I asked. We were in a lonely-looking, long corridor, with cameras on the walls, and many doors all looking the same.

'This,' I was told, 'is your new room.'

'On my own? *Between* the boys and girls?' I was in a staff room in a corridor between two wings, in splendid isolation. I had watched the Berlin Wall come down and Nelson Mandela walk free from jail – but now I was in a literal no-man's land, through no fault of my own. I couldn't even leave the room at night to go to the bathroom otherwise the alarms in the corridor would go off. A bucket, which I refused to use, was my emergency chamber pot.

I never saw my dad again. Mum eventually won custody

of my brother and sister and they moved with her into sheltered accommodation. There wasn't enough room or money for me, so this was going to be my home for the foreseeable future until Mum was better sorted out. She couldn't come and visit because the unit was a long way from home and Mum, who I would eventually find out had become an alcoholic and would never be fit enough to take me back, had neither money nor a car.

I was assigned a key worker and met her in a small room just a few doors down from my cell.

'Hi, I'm Debbie,' she said, reaching out for my hand, the first person to offer me this symbol of potential friendship. She had big, red-framed glasses, wild curly hair and loved nothing more than to dance pagan rituals on the fields of southern England. Debbie, who believed in guardian spirits, was just the person for me. She was the only person who talked to me like she talked to everyone else. Normally when anyone spoke to me, they put on a special tone like they were addressing someone who was mentally disabled or someone they found disgusting. I quizzed her about her dancing and then, more significantly, about the guardian spirits.

'What are these guardian spirits then, Debbie?'

'They are angels sent to look after us here on earth.'

'Well, where's mine then?'

'They are here. I can see your aura is damaged, you should meditate, let the spirits in and heal you.'

'Whatever, Debbie,' I said laughing. 'You're mad.'

'Try it, sweetheart.'

I thought it was ridiculous but there was something in Debbie's expression, not pity, but sincerity. She really believed some salvation would come my way if I did what she said. I liked the idea of guardian angels, of someone watching over me the whole time who would never abandon me. And so, from that night, I started to meditate, to think and then dream of my angels, and for the first time I felt a little less lonely in my solitary cell as I drifted off to sleep.

'I'm sorry, Johnny, there's nothing I can do. I've got to move on.'

I cried, demanding that Debbie stay for me, accusing her of hating me by leaving. But I was powerless. Her child was sick and she had to be near a specialist hospital in another city. I was hard on her, a reflection of just how much she meant to me.

I had spent eighteen months (so much for temporary) in this nightmare place and I thought I had started to win the respect of the staff. As a result of my improved behaviour and enjoyment of study, I was chosen to go, as the best-behaved boy, along with the best-behaved girl, who was seventeen years old, to a party in a private house.

We were driven there in a minibus, practically jumping in excitement – this was my first party, I couldn't wait. But after we walked through the front door and were swathed in smoke and deafened by dance music, it turned out everyone was on drugs or drunk and, even worse, orgies were taking place in some of the rooms. I ran from the house and hid in the minibus. Two members of the female care home staff were there. We thought we were lucky to be going on that trip but, instead, our reward for good behaviour was supposed to be joining in with the drugs and sexual abuse. I had a lucky escape. The girl stayed inside and I have no idea what happened to her in there. She didn't answer when I asked her and she said nothing on the trip back to the unit.

Then, suddenly, it was announced that, as my mum wasn't able to look after me, they had found me a foster family. The other kids teased me, saying they were real weirdos; they had to be to take me.

'You know what happened to the last kid they had?' Darren asked.

'No, what?'

'Jumped in front of a train.'

They were extremely religious. The man, Eric, tall, potbellied and balding, was a minister, and his wife, Barbara, a thin, dark-haired woman with a pointy chin and nose, quoted the Bible at me whenever I said or did some-thing wrong, or had the wrong expression on my face (which was all the time).

Barbara was always saying something about how 'Man born of woman, is short-lived and full of pain.' Well I was a woman born of a woman who everyone thought was a man but I wasn't about to go into that with these two crackpots. They also said I was full of evil spirits and they were going to rid me of them. This involved prayer and sapping my will through starvation. I didn't know why they wanted to foster kids because it was clear to me that they didn't like kids at all.

When the social worker came to see me, she squinted for a long time before writing lots of notes in a file on her clip-board. Why did she have to write so much? It wasn't as if I was saying anything.

I lived off Cup-a-Soups from a vending machine at school (the only thing I could afford from the so-called lunch money my foster parents gave me). I'd already thinned out quite a bit at the unit but now I started to disappear into my clothes. My belt tightened up a notch, then two, then three.

The next time the social worker came, she looked me in the eye and said: 'How long have you been anorexic?' I didn't have the courage to say that I was full of evil spirits and these lovely people were starving me to get rid of them. I dreaded being taken back – at least here I was allowed to go to a normal school (not that school's much fun when you're starving all the time).

I came home one day to find Eric waiting at the top of the stairs.

'Come here.'

I walked up, bag over my shoulder, feeling dizzy as I reached the top.

Eric raised a copy of the *Gay Times*. 'What's this?' he demanded.

'None of your bloody business!'

This mag was about my most precious possession, hidden under my mattress. I was furious that Eric had been through my room and raged as he, with the most righteous of expressions, berated the evil spirits in me that had turned me into a homosexual.

I reached for the magazine to take it back but Eric snapped it away, holding it up over his head like he was the Statue of Liberty, and pushed me back. But for the lack of food I might have kept my balance or caught the banister but instead the world blurred, my limbs flailed and I fell backwards on to the stairs and rolled down, arse over tea-kettle. I slammed into the front door with a bang and just knew I had to get out, just as I had known to run from Dad before I was seriously hurt. Barbara appeared and starting spitting her religious nonsense at me.

I stumbled to my feet and screamed: 'You're a stupid, fucking, crazy bitch who wouldn't know Jesus if he slapped you in the face!' and ran out the front door.

It was almost two years to the day since I'd run out of my family home. It was freezing and foggy and I headed for the city. It was too cold to sleep on the streets so I kept walking, blue-nosed, until I saw a hospital and snuck into A&E. A police officer shook me awake at dawn. 'Come on.' No chance to pee or wash my face and we were off to another care home, but not before the final humiliation in front of a social worker. Eric and Barbara had told social services I had abused them verbally before attacking them. In response I pulled off my T-shirt and turned around. My malnourished body was covered in red marks and bruises from where I'd fallen down the stairs. I was so angry but I couldn't speak. I didn't know what to say. The social worker said and did nothing except fill out the paperwork, a literal box-ticking exercise, then made some calls and drove me to another care home. This latest one was a bit more like a normal house, but it was too little, too late. A pattern had been set now. When things got too much, which was often, when my well of loneliness seemed bottomless (which was almost all of the time), I just walked out and stayed out.

I was walking the streets randomly one night when a car

slid up alongside me. The window wound down and a woman's voice said: 'You all right, love? You look cold. Why don't you come with us? Sit in the car for a bit, we'll put some music on. Got lots of CDs.'

I glanced inside and saw a smiling young woman with large earrings, wearing a black leather jacket and smoking a cigarette. There was indeed a large selection of CDs spread out over the dashboard. I was freezing and could feel the warmth of the car pouring out. I couldn't face walking away from that wonderful heat and so I shrugged and got in. They took me to a nice-looking house, although it was quite bare inside, hardly any furniture, just a double bed in the back room with a TV and video player.

'Stay here,' the man said. Minutes later, two men came in and put a video cassette on the player. It was gay porn. We talked for a bit as they watched; our chat was all very friendly. They shared their smokes and drinks, and told me how beautiful I was. I was really skinny and had long dark hair. I was fourteen but looked a lot younger. I wanted to believe we were going to be friends but the conversation turned sexual and, although I told myself I wanted to do this for friendship and I did not resist, the men took turns raping me.

The care home knew what was going on. The couple picked me up and dropped me off there almost every night. They gave me CDs for my trouble. There were only four other kids in the home but I wasn't into speaking to anyone else. I just wanted to escape and, as I soon as I could on my sixteenth birthday, I signed myself out of the care home.

The couple had once taken me to a house occupied by squatters who said I could live there once I got out of the home. They'd been evicted but I quickly found them by hanging out near a pub I knew they liked to go to and they kept their promise, giving me my own room in a large house, which was dry but lacked hot water or heating. They'd bypassed the meter to get electric, so we had light and small electric heaters were running in some of the rooms.

They were punks and didn't particularly care what anyone did or what they looked like. We were united by the fact we were misfits, society aliens, so I started to live as a woman and felt, for the first time, as though I were free. No one would have guessed I was a boy. I could tell from the looks I got from both men and boys that I was a good-looking girl.

I signed on for income support and found out I might be eligible for a fashion design course at the local college. It seemed as though, despite everything, I still had a brain, because they let me in. Things were looking up.

I was walking back from college to the squat one evening when I noticed a large group of boys behind me. They started calling me 'poofter' and when I replied that they all must fancy me because they were following me down the street, they gave chase. I ran but my heels were no match for their Reeboks, so they quickly caught up with me. They beat me to the ground. As the boots and fists came in, unable to catch my breath to even cry out, I knew then I could never be a woman and survive.

If I had to be a man then I would go all the way. I changed my clothes and shaved my head before my wounds had healed. And then I discovered the gay clubs – great congregations of gay people, a wonderful world, safe at last in a place I could almost be myself. I lived in these clubs, it was where I would spend all my time, every day that I could.

A tap on my shoulder while in the club and I turned and found myself looking at the handsomest man I'd ever seen – muscular, good height, tough-looking.

'My name's Simon. Can I buy you a drink?' I was smitten. We went home together. He stayed the next day. We went out again that night. The next day was the same. I couldn't believe that this man, who was thirty-two, double my age, wanted to love me, to be with me.

Between the gay clubs and Simon I was in heaven. I wanted to be like this always. But after two months of bliss he said, 'I don't want to be gay. I'm not gay. *You* made me do this.'

He said he'd been in a relationship with a woman before he met me. I was the first 'man' he'd ever had sex with. I could believe it. He was hard as anything, couldn't appear more heterosexual, and as if to prove it he told me: 'Anyone finds out about this, you're dead.'

I promised him then that I was going to become a woman and then he could take my virginity, something he became obsessed with. But my change wouldn't happen overnight – I hadn't the first clue how to go about it, so he upped and left, returning to his woman and abandoning me.

It was as if a meteorite had destroyed my world. I couldn't eat or sleep and was in so much pain that within a few days of Simon leaving me, I took an overdose. I woke up in hospital and, as soon as I was coherent, social services put me back into a secure unit. I ran away that night to look for Simon, to find drugs, and survived by selling my body for cash. I lived like that until social services managed to find me a Leaving Care flat in a house run by a homophobic man called Steve who couldn't keep the disgust from his face whenever he talked to me. Steve just shrugged when I told him some skinheads had put fireworks through my door, like it was tough, I'd brought it upon myself by being gay.

I tried to find a way out, though. First, I signed up for the Youth Training Scheme in fashion and then set about hitting the clubs every night I could manage. At one club I met a good-looking guy in his thirties. He said he was a doctor and he invited me back to his place, which turned out to be a large detached house on a quiet suburban street.

As we drew near, the 'doctor' started giving off a strange vibe. I should have run right then. When we stepped into the broad hallway, he asked me to take my shoes off; he said he'd just had the house re-carpeted in this expensive, plush carpet.

'It's like walking on fur,' he said, as we removed our shoes. He opened the door to the lounge, saying, 'After you.' I already had a sense that other people were in the house as I stepped through, and had just a moment to acclimatise to some bright lights before I saw a group of half a dozen men standing in a half circle and a video camera in the middle of the room. 'Wow, you're beautiful,' said a small potbellied man in his forties. I didn't hesitate. I ran to the front window, slid it up and leapt out, running down the road in my socks.

I eventually got a tenancy of my first flat in another town where I studied massage on the Youth Training

Scheme and worked in a nursing home. I spent all my time at work or on the many buses I had to take to get around, so there was little chance to go clubbing, although I had no trouble finding boyfriends. I treated them badly and was physically and verbally abusive, just to get a reaction. I was a mess; I'd sleep with people for all the wrong reasons. Sex was sometimes a bit of a disaster, depending on the type of guy I pulled. I could only be on the receiving end, I didn't have the tackle, so I couldn't go with men who wanted to be the female, and I made sure that those relationships remained platonic.

I'd only ever loved Simon, the one man who'd treated me like a girl. I thought about him every day and searched the clubs each night looking for him before deciding I was going to be like him. I started going to the gym and getting tattoos done – this was how guys I liked looked.

Eventually I ran away again, running to London without money or a job – just bleached hair, a wiry physique and the clothes I was in. Cut loose in the world's wildest city, where trouble waited around every corner.

AMANDA

Memories of my own mum are never far away. One day at work at a refuge I was suddenly overcome with sadness and anger. Angry with myself for blaming my mum for having to sell her own body – and thereby her spirit and her soul – to survive. As I vowed to make mental amends to my mum when I got home, Amanda approached me.

'I'm on my way to see social services,' she said. 'I'm going to read my files.'

I couldn't help but wonder if she was ready. Seeing your past laid out in an aged folder is more traumatic than you might imagine. Long-forgotten memories can come crashing back in mighty waves that can leave you psychologically devastated.

'I know what you're thinking,' Amanda said, seeing my expression. 'I know I'm ready.'

Mum and Dad split up when I was still a toddler. Even though Dad was only in his early twenties, he had two families on the go, with a total of six kids, two in ours and four in the other, and he chose the other family over my older brother, Mum and me, which was understandable, considering my mum really was a nightmare to live with.

To be fair, she was extremely young, just sixteen years old when she had me. Dad was twenty-one and left not long after I arrived – I was just another noisy mouth to feed adding to the stress.

Mum liked to drink a *lot*, preferably in company and preferably at a sleazy pub or club. To that end, she'd depart the house as darkness fell, leaving me and Jack, who was older by eighteen months, home alone while she spent the night on the town, partying and drinking.

Apparently, we woke each other one night, after one of us had a nightmare, and we screamed so long and loud that the neighbour called the cops, who kicked the door in and followed up by calling social services.

The social services got Mum some help, a volunteer who babysat – but not at night and not so Mum could go out drinking, which is what she did. Mum was caught out again when she was arrested for fighting over something to do with her new boyfriend, who had been in and out of prison for a number of violent offences. The police brought her home and found me and Jack – he was four, I was two-and-a-half. Once again, we were screaming the flat down.

Reading all that back now, I can see how social services thought that if we were left in her care, there was a good chance we wouldn't make it past our fifth birthdays.

Things were so bad that I actually told a social worker that I didn't want to go home and be with Mum, so we were fostered a few times, but that didn't really work out. At one place the foster parents started to hit us and so I responded with a dirty protest, wiping my poo on the walls, and that was enough to get us removed. The foster carers who had abused us weren't investigated.

After that, fostering stalled for us, so we were taken to live in a children's home run by nuns. The building was a Victorian school with gothic tendencies, which was scary enough, but when I was greeted by an Irish nun who also happened to be albino, I almost wet myself. The albino nun was nothing compared to my roommate, Violet, who sat on the edge of the bed, murmuring a ritual phrase I was never able to hear, as she rocked herself to sleep at night. Christ only knows what she'd been through. I know all she deserved was love and sympathy but, being an anxious five-year-old, I did all I could to avoid interacting with this spooky child. I spent my first few weeks mostly petrified. I begged to be put in a room with Jack but he was down the hall, in the boys' dormitory, and the nuns couldn't bring themselves to make an exception.

The nuns were kind. They gave us lots of hugs and did their best to comfort me. I was thrown into a state of anxiety when one smiling sister told me: 'Your Mum's coming to visit, Amanda. Won't that be nice?'

No it would not. I had given up on Mum; I knew she was full of shit. She only involved us when she needed something like a new council flat and so she made a show of trying to get her life back on track to ensure she got it.

Her visits were full of fake affection and, when the nuns left us alone, she turned on the bitchiness and, alongside digs at my lack of delight to see her, she went on about how awful I looked. She was one to talk. Her hair was a multitude of uneven brown and blonde stripes, her lips bright red, eyelashes long, thick and black, and eyeshadow a shade even a graffiti artist would have put back on the shelf.

The nuns could see that my mum's visits left me deeply disturbed and, while they did their best to make me feel better, there was only so much they could do.

I felt so alone; so alone, in fact, that I had a nervous breakdown. My mum had left me feeling so lost and confused, I prayed to God in the church we went to every Sunday and at night from my window, from where I could see the church, that she would undergo a miraculous change, like the caterpillar into a butterfly, and that my life would make sense. God failed to answer my prayers, so I stopped believing in him, which broke my heart because I trusted the lovely stories I'd been told about this wonderful being who watched over us all and cared for us all so much.

I was loud, boisterous and temperamental. I didn't make friends. I only wanted to play with my brother. Thanks to Mum I had a huge and rude vocabulary and every other word started with 'f' or 's'. I had little interest in study and was behind with reading, writing and maths. If there was one word that summed me up at the time it was angry. I was five years old and furious with the world, but it was impossible for me to put that into words, or to get to grips with my feelings. I didn't understand that my anger came from sadness.

* * *

Bill and Celia became our foster parents when I was six years old. The nuns had been struggling to find Jack and me a place and had suggested splitting us up and, true to form, I said: 'No fucking way!'

So they looked further afield and, after we had interest from Bill and Celia, things moved quickly. We were allowed a day together to see how we'd get on and they took us on a visit to London Zoo which, naturally, blew both our minds. From king-size pythons to tigers, and from penguins to monkeys – well, if wonders like this were waiting for us in the real world, then I would gladly accept Bill and Celia as my mum and dad.

It had taken me a few weeks to get used to the albino nun, but I'd since come to love her; she was the most patient and kind lady of them all when it came to taking care of me. As she put me to bed after our zoo visit, I begged her to let Bill and Celia take us. I don't know how much influence she had but that's just what happened.

My faith in God was restored, just a little.

Bill and Celia took us home, to a lovely warm house in Colchester, where we had our own rooms. 'Dad' told us he was a soldier and that meant he had to go away for long stretches at a time but that he would always come back and 'Mum' would look after us in the meantime.

Bill was quite chubby for a soldier, aged about forty and I think he only got us because Celia made him. They couldn't have children of their own and, while Bill might have been content to go through life childless, Celia demanded children.

I also learned that Bill seemed to have a calming effect on Celia, that there were two sides to her personality.

They had been warned about our behavioural problems and had been forgiving, kissing us good night and good morning, always with a smile but, the day after Bill left, Celia turned into the Wicked Witch of the West. She even looked like her, with her long pointy nose and crazy, thin-lipped, evil mouth. She had tight-curled, black hair and huge, round glasses the size of jam-jar lids that made her eyes look enormous.

Celia still demanded good morning and good night kisses from us each day but now without a smile, without a trace of warmth. She was cold, distant, punishing and cruel – vicious. We were terrified by her temper. Even Jack, normally afraid of nothing, jumped out of his skin when Celia suddenly screamed at him because the dog was ill and she wanted to know what he'd done to him to make him sick. When he protested his innocence, Celia turned to me. We hadn't done anything but that didn't stop Celia from tying us up on the landing, fastening us to door handles with elastic bands while spouting religious nonsense about how we were going to go to hell unless we buckled down and became good little children.

Relief came after about three months, when Bill returned from the army and Celia's parents joined us for Christmas. They were lovely and, in a rare few days of utter joy, they came armed, along with Bill, with a whole child's bedroom-worth of presents. My favourite gift was the roller skates and I made the most of this happy time, while Celia played along with her parents and Bill. Only Jack and I knew about the nutter behind this facade.

Bill was given a new posting in the New Year and we

moved to an army camp in Cumbria. We lived on a base that was all prefab houses, blasted concrete roads with not a tree anywhere in sight. The sky was always grey and even when the sun did shine, the dull, brown, scrubby landscape swallowed the light whole. It was miles from any village, let alone town, and social services stopped coming because it was so far off the beaten track. We stayed here for an unbelievably bleak two-and-a-half years, during which time Bill was hardly ever at home. He was constantly on exercises or training for something or other. I think he just wanted to get away from us all.

Even when our birth Mum wanted to come see us, pushed by some unknown motive, she found the distance too great. It was like being trapped on a very boring desert island with a crazy woman who had violent tendencies. We were always on edge as we never knew what she would do from one moment to the next. Even our school was in this camp and the teacher couldn't cope with our erratic behaviour. Celia, not surprisingly, had no friends. It was just us and her. I had no idea why she wanted kids. I felt so helpless when she hit Jack, there was nothing I could do to stop her – we still had to kiss her first thing in the morning and last thing at night and it was terrifying, she always looked so fierce and some-times when we turned our faces up, ready to kiss her, she slapped us.

Early on, a couple of months after this nightmare began, we travelled to court where we were to be officially adopted. As part of the procedure the social worker asked me if I really wanted to stay with Bill and Celia. I said I did because I didn't know what else to do. The social worker assumed everything was perfect, that this was a happy ending to her case. I didn't think I could say no, and the same went for Jack.

Five years after the adoption hearing, when I was ten years old, Bill told us he wanted to leave the army and move to the coast somewhere south. To that end, we moved from Cumbria to a camp in West Sussex where Jack and I slept on camp beds. Most of the furniture in our old house had belonged to the army and so we were living in a temporary house while Bill looked for somewhere along the Sussex coast.

The first week we were there, I struggled to get to sleep most evenings. After a few restless nights, I woke up with my nightie around my neck and a pain down below. When I opened my eyes I was looking into Bill's face. He made a 'Shhh' motion and continued to abuse me. From that day on, Bill abused me once every single week.

I was in hell. I had this woman on my case all day and then at night this man, who I once had seen as my saviour, the man who was able to pacify Celia the Wicked Witch, was now an abuser.

We moved to an amazing house in a town right by the sea. There was a big garden and sand dunes rolled down towards the beach. The school was great and I was allowed to go horse riding. The whole town was middle-class and conservative with a small 'c'.

For the first time in my life I fell in love with school and the kids that went there. So this was what it was like to live in the normal world! But the nice surroundings couldn't guard me from the life I'd lived up until then. When I was thirteen, I started to become interested in dressing in a more adult style, and using make-up – as well as becoming interested in boys.

I started to climb out of my window in the evening, which accomplished two things: it stopped the abuse and I was able to hang out with older boys. I grew more confident as my hormones kicked in and, one night, I was ready when Bill came in. I demanded he stop abusing me. That if he didn't I was going to tell my boyfriends and they were going to beat him up and then I would go to the police and tell them exactly what he'd done to me once a week for the past four years.

Bill took this calmly, then came up with a compromise – he'd make me watch porn and touch myself. He would leave the room while I did this and then come back in and check my pulse.

'And when you want to start having sex,' he told me, 'just let me know.'

I had to get out of there. I worked three jobs: a paper round, a bakery assistant and a waitress. Apart from being able to save money, this meant I could spend as much time as possible out of the house.

I started seeing a boy, Tommy, who was a bit older than me, after he asked me to slow dance at a disco. We went out for a year and a half, only ever kissing. I really fell for him and experienced love for the first time – I had no idea such powerful emotions existed.

Life at home hadn't changed. Jack was doing OK. He was almost sixteen and too big for Celia to abuse now and wouldn't take any nonsense. Jack was just as messed up as me, mentally and emotionally, however. I really wanted to leave. I had to cycle five miles to one of my jobs and one night, as I was about to leave work at midnight and begin my hour-long pedal home, I thought, 'I can't take living in that house any more.' So I stole some money from the restaurant where I worked, got a taxi to the train station and caught the last train to Brighton.

The police picked me up. They didn't take me seriously at all, chuckling as they said: 'You've been a naughty girl, haven't you?'

'I'm not going back home,' I told them. And I said that my step-dad was abusing me. They didn't believe me.

'You're going to have to go home,' one officer replied.

I lost it. I screamed, 'No I'm not!' over and over until they let me talk some more and then agreed to put me in a place of safety – which turned out to be a caravan in Worthing.

The next day I made an official statement, detailing the abuse. They still didn't believe me. As far as they were concerned, I'd stolen money, so therefore I was a trouble-maker. They tried to talk me out of it but I'd made up my mind. Whatever it took, whatever anyone said, I wasn't going to live with Bill and Celia any more.

So they interviewed Bill.

The officers' faces had changed when they came back in to talk to me.

'What?' I asked.

Bill had said, on tape, that he'd squeezed my breasts a few times, but only because I'd asked him to, because I wanted him to. He'd also said I'd asked him to do a lot more and accused me of being a seductress.

This was the typical response of a paedophile unused

to police interviews – a glimpse into how their twisted minds work.

'I'm sorry we didn't believe you,' the officer said. 'You won't be going back there.'

While I waited for the court case I was put into temporary foster care with an old couple who lived in the middle of nowhere. They had a teenage son with learning difficulties who was a chronic masturbator. I had to listen to him go at it every night as my room was next door and the walls were paper-thin.

'Even a children's home would be better than this,' I told my social worker, and so that's where I ended up, in a house in Lewes, just in time for my fifteenth birthday.

Jack said he'd decided to stay with Bill and Celia. Bill had never abused him and now he was able to handle Celia, he wanted to finish school and then decide what he was going to do.

In the run-up to the court case I was asked to go to a meeting with Bill and Celia. I think they were hoping they could talk me into dropping the charges. As soon as Bill started speaking I stopped him, stating: 'This is bullshit,' and walked out of the room.

I developed full-blown symptoms of post-traumatic stress disorder (PTSD) – an extreme type of anxiety disorder that sometimes develops in people after they've suffered or witnessed traumatic events. I was in a constant state of hyper-awareness – 'danger mode' – and couldn't switch off. I yelled at people for the stupidest thing, exploded every time I spoke to someone official. To the inexperienced staff at the care home, I was a real pain in the backside, a crazy person. What they didn't realise was that this was a result of the accumulation of years of damage.

I really started to abuse alcohol, drinking until I passed out, waking without any memory of what had taken place the night before.

Sam was the only worker who had some sense of how to talk to me. He held me one night, when I was about to try and hang myself, and was firm but fair with me during my rages, talking to me, showing me reason, until I calmed down. But Sam wasn't a trained therapist and so the PTSD continued to wreak havoc with my life until I was sixteen and I finally went to court to face that bastard Bill and his bitch of a wife. My barrister came to see me a week before the trial was due to start.

'Your step-father is willing to admit to a lesser charge,' he said. 'Consensual sex with a girl over thirteen.' This was a typical defence ploy. If I admitted that I'd led Bill on, the court would sympathise and, as I was over thirteen, the sentencing for sexual abuse is much lighter. Apparently, according to the courts, it's much worse to rape a twelve-year-old than it is to rape a thirteen-year-old. There was no way I was ever going to agree to something like that.

'No, that's a lie,' I told the barrister. 'I want to go to court and tell everyone the truth.'

I had to stand up in front of everyone and tell them what Bill had done. I'm sure he was counting on me not being able to, or falling apart under cross-examination, which I thought was never going to end. The case was reported in the papers, where he was named and shamed. I held firm and spoke clearly, although it was hard to speak about some aspects, as I had to use the 'polite' names for everything.

The jury believed me and Bill was found guilty on four counts. The verdict was unanimous. He was given a nine-month suspended sentence. I couldn't believe it. For what he'd done? That was all? Barely a slap on the wrist.

Sam helped me so much to get through this, along with my English teacher, Paul, who was really posh but lovely. They were both in their twenties and showed belief in me, that I would be able to do something positive with my life, even when I was at my absolute lowest. These two men were my first positive experiences outside of the nuns' home and they gave me hope; something in me clicked on to the idea that not everyone was bad.

For me, social workers were the enemy and not to be trusted under any circumstances. They were desperate to get rid of you as fast as they possibly could so they could get on to their next hopeless case. I was due to move out of the children's home as I approached eighteen and one social worker had the bright idea of trying to persuade me to see my mum. The last time I'd seen her was when I was seven; they just didn't seem to get it. My mum didn't give a toss about me. Why would I want to see her now? How on earth was she supposed to make me feel better about anything?

Instead, I applied for a place in supported lodgings run by a young Christian couple, Dai and Marie. They meant well but they'd bitten off far more than they could chew with me. I was out at all hours and by now had discovered other drugs besides alcohol and cigarettes. I was making Angel Delight in the kitchen one night when Marie came downstairs in her nightie.

'What the hell do you think you're doing?' Marie demanded.

Angel Delight is supposed to be the simplest thing you could ever make but there was powder and milk all over the kitchen and I seemed to have used about five pots to try and mix it. I was very stoned.

'Don't you know what time it is?'

I stared at the kitchen clock. 'Four o'clock,' I replied.

'In the bloody morning!'

Oh, they tried, they really tried. But I drank all their wine and sold the TV they bought for me to have in my room. And after I agreed to one last chance, I stole Marie's engagement ring, pawned it and used the money to buy weed and alcohol. Marie had already called the housing officer so she could start looking for other potential places for me. I was high and told the housing officer what I'd done when we were alone. She got me to show her where I'd sold the ring and she bought it back for Marie.

After that I was moved to a B&B. The people were nice, once again; they were a gay couple, Malcolm and Terry, but I didn't give a damn. I was either high, taking speed and ecstasy, or trying to get high. Again I sold the TV they'd put in my room. They replaced it, which surprised me. They also cooked me a meal every evening. I did grow to like them and was trying to at least respect their home, until I arrived one Sunday night to find no meal waiting. Terry was stretched out on the sofa with a crazy headache that he said was giving him visions. The doctor had scheduled a brain scan for the following day but the tumour that was pressing on Terry's brain killed him that night. It was a narrow, four-storey house and I looked down from my room on the top floor as the body bag was carried out on the ambulance stretcher. Just when I had hopes of settling down, a place and people I could respect, this had happened.

So, I cursed God and really let loose.

TINA

Tina is a good friend of mine, someone I can go to when I need to open up, when my own memories threaten to overwhelm me. When I asked Tina if she was prepared to share her own story for this book, I really wasn't sure that she'd agree. I knew her story but had never heard her tell it all in one go before, from beginning to end. As we talked, the tea growing cold, Tina told me that today was the anniversary of her mother's death and it was good for her to talk, to keep her mother's memory alive. I was reminded – as I so often have to be - that I was not the only one haunted by tragedy. Life moves on but sometimes it moves on before we're ready.

Mum was my rock. No two ways about it. She was hard but fair, always. Hardest when needs be and loveliest when needs be; she disciplined me and wiped away my tears. She taught me right from wrong and was my best friend. She ran her own business, selling office fixtures and fittings, and this had toughened her physically (from constantly moving stock) and mentally (having to survive in a male-dominated world, she always said you have to be twice as good at your job as the best man was at his). She was in her fifties and fitter than many people half her age, me included, although I had the excuse that I was eight months pregnant with my second daughter, Emily, so was hardly in a position to exercise. Sophie, my other daughter, was just coming up to six. It was the end of the summer holidays and she was just about to go back to school in a few days. I needed to get her some shoes for school and told Mum I was off to get them. Sophie didn't want to come with me, it was a lovely, sunny September day, and the hours were precious before she had to buckle down to the hard work of school. Mum was inside, hoovering, singing 'I Want to Break Free', which cracked us both up.

I tried Sophie one more time. 'Sure you don't want to come, sweetheart?'

'No, Mum, I'll stay here with Gran.'

I gave Sophie a kiss and waved to her friend Briony. 'Be good girls.'

I'd made it as far as the bus stop when I realised I'd forgotten my purse on Mum's kitchen table, so I turned around, waved at the kids playing and went inside. Something was wrong. The hoover was off and just lying in the lounge, the snake-like neck coiled on the floor any old way. That wasn't like Mum. Plus, it was so quiet; I couldn't hear any movement.

'Mum?'

A voice barely audible came from the stair landing. 'Up here.'

She was so pale, it was like looking at the living dead, her eyes were open but her face was so gaunt. 'I don't feel well.'

'Lie down, Mum,' I told her and helped her to the bed. 'Your skin's so cold; let me get you a hot water bottle, OK?'

She nodded and lay on the bed, breathing heavily. 'So glad you're here,' she said. 'I didn't think you'd get back in time.'

'Just rest, Mum,' I said, finding the hot water bottle in the bottom drawer of the chest. 'I'll get you this and then we'd better call the doctor.'

I was downstairs filling the kettle when I heard the softest of moans and ran back up. 'Mum, are you all right?' I knew the moment I saw her that she was dead.

I went into labour two days after I buried my mother. I was a single mum without a mum of my own. I had a six-year-old girl and a brand new baby daughter. My rock was gone and I was adrift on an unfamiliar and terrifying sea. Two days after giving birth, I was home and paralysed. I couldn't get out of bed. I felt like nothing mattered but I knew that if I didn't do something this baby wasn't going to get brought up. So I called someone and bought some speed. It wasn't hard to find. I wasn't a drug user but I knew what speed was supposed to do – it was a pick-me-up, a get-up-and-go drug. I lived in a small town and it was easy enough to find a friend of a friend who put me in touch with the right person.

It gave me enough of an energy boost to get me out of bed and take care of the kids. When the kids weren't in the house, I just sat there like a dummy, smoking, doing nothing, even when the speed was racing in my veins. The only thing I liked to do was work in the garden, weeding like a maniac because that was something that Mum liked to do, although I nearly had a breakdown when one of the plants died. Mum would never have let that happen.

I'd split up with the girls' father, Liam, not long after I'd fallen pregnant with Emily. He was a drinker and had turned violent a couple of times. He hadn't wanted kids and although he now said he wanted to be a good father, he wasn't much of one, although it was nice to let him play with the girls so I could stare blankly into space for a while, the TV on but not watching it. When he then made a move on me one night, I let the blankness stay and it was the night of all nights, a night when I could conceive and conceive I did. That guy was fertile. He just had to wave at women and they fell pregnant. When I found out I was pregnant, my first thought was that I didn't want the baby. My second thought was how bad a person I was to think such a thing. After that, I took some speed and let the baby be an 'it'. I put 'it' to one side of my mind, shoved 'it' under a corner like dirty socks under a pile of dirty laundry, as if 'it' wasn't there. I took speed all the way through my pregnancy and the months shot by, it was as if my pregnancy lasted nine days, not nine months. Months spent sitting on the sofa in between feeding and sorting out the girls.

I'd taken drugs during the day in the run-up to giving birth, but not while I was in the hospital. Liam had the girls for the duration and I trusted his mum to take care of them for a couple of days. I just wanted to make sure I got out of there as fast as possible; before they found out I was an addict. I pretended everything was all OK, when it clearly wasn't. After I'd given birth, there was no rush of love at all, which made me feel awful, like I didn't deserve to be a mum. It wasn't until the following day that her squeals broke my glassy stare out of the window across a car park. She hadn't been feeding properly and so the nurses were putting a feeding tube in her nose; I could see her inside a room with glass windows and as she squealed I cried out, 'That's my baby!' The mother instinct had kicked in. She was my little angel – Angie.

Liam moved in with me after I got out of the hospital but he was drinking a lot. I didn't feel like I could tell him off; after all, I was using six grammes of speed a day – a lethal dose to a non-user – and so I was hiding things as bad as he was. No one knew about my addiction – I kept it from everybody. I always carried the speed on me and never, ever used if there was a chance someone could see me.

Liam couldn't cope with me and the kids. He was a child himself. All I wanted to talk about was my wonderful mum and Liam started to snap more and more often, beating me until the police were called. After the fifth time they made Liam move out for twenty-four hours to calm down and then, when I was alone with the police, they asked me if I wanted to press charges. They were lovely, really, up until this point. Perhaps they'd waited until things were bad enough before pressing me to do something about it but I said I didn't.

'Don't you want to change things?' the young male

officer asked me. 'For your kids?' I just looked down at my feet and waited for them to leave. 'You have a duty of care to your children and you're failing them with that man around the house,' the officer continued. 'That means you come under our duty of care. Do you understand?' They told me a social worker would come by in a few days.

My kids were clean and well fed. But I was using fourteen grammes on my very worst day. I was doing what I needed to do for the kids but nothing more. The house had become messy and the kids had adapted – it had become normal to them to reuse dirty clothes because I hadn't done the washing. Sophie turned into a mum to Emily and Angie as I watched from inside my speed bubble, thinking that this shouldn't be happening. Every night of every day I'd think tomorrow will be the day I'll do something – and eight hours later I'd still be sitting in my dressing gown, licking my finger and swabbing up the last grains of speed from the little paper wrap, which is what I was doing when the doorbell rang and I found a smiling stranger on my doorstep who introduced herself as Mary, my social worker.

My mum and dad had children with different partners before they had me, both of them girls. When they had me, my eldest sister, Madge, was three and she was Dad's; Steph, aged two, was Mum's. Dad was a gambler, the sort that would bet the last 50p we had put aside for the electricity meter. Mum, being a strong-minded woman, told Dad to leave. She would raise us three kids without him. Then he was free to waste his life on gambling.

I was three when social services turned up at Granddad's house. By the time Mum arrived, all Granddad could say through the tears was, 'They've gone.'

Dad had told social services that Mum was always going out at night, seeing other men, leaving the kids alone, and for some unknown reason they had taken him at his word.

Dad had decided that if he couldn't have us kids then no one could. This had nothing to do with his love for us; it was just pure bitter selfishness of a warped gambling mind – all or nothing. He should have known by then that double or quits was always a losing proposition.

We didn't see Mum for a long time. It was hard for her to visit because she had to go to three different addresses. We had been split up and were in different foster homes. Mum was tough, but tears crept out of her eyes every time she saw us. She'd tried, oh she'd tried so hard to get us back, she said. I believed her. Madge did not. She hated Mum and blamed her for us ending up in care.

Dad got Madge out of care within a couple of years. Madge only realised that Dad had lied and that Mum had loved her when we met by chance, on the school bus. She was fifteen years old.

I'd always believed Mum and Mum had managed to get me back when I was five.

By the time Madge and I had realised who we were, she was desperate to see Mum.

'I need to sit down,' was all Mum said when I told her. When she had her breath again, she asked me what Madge was like.

'She's lovely, Mum, and she really wants to see you.'

Madge came around two days later, fell in Mum's arms and sobbed and sobbed. They fell in love all over again.

Mum was so happy, so happy. She cried but told me these were tears of joy, not of sadness.

'I hate Dad for what he did to us,' Madge said.

'Let's put that behind us now, OK?' Mum said. 'I just want to be part of your life again.'

Steph was very different. Madge just wanted to be loved but Steph was bitter, was really hurting and still blamed Mum. And she was jealous that I'd been with Mum longer. She was really hurt and confused. Dad had remarried and Steph and Madge were both living with him.

We were all angry kids. Dad had had the audacity to do something like this, but wasn't man enough to admit his mistakes. But once Madge knew, I think he had no choice but to come and see Mum. Madge told me what she'd told Dad: 'Mum's a lovely lady; I really hate you for what you've done. You destroyed Mum.'

I was just home from school, setting my homework up when there was a knock at the door. I peered out of my window.

'Mum, there's a strange man at the door.' I watched as he walked around to the back door that opened into the kitchen where Mum was. He knocked. Mum opened it and froze.

'What the fuck do you want?'

'I've come to say sorry.'

'You despicable, lying bastard. A sledgehammer to my head would have been nicer. But take my kids? How very fucking dare you?'

I thought Mum was going to kill him; I'd never heard her talk with such anger in her voice. Dad couldn't look Mum in the eye.

'What's the matter?' she said. 'Guilt got the better of you?'

I'd stayed in the hallway listening but, not wanting to be seen, I retreated quietly upstairs to my bedroom. Then I heard their voices getting louder and got worried, so I went back downstairs.

The way Mum spoke was like nothing I'd ever heard, it was so final and from the heart.

'I'm going to tell you exactly what I think of you.'

I think there was something wrong with Dad; I could tell it wasn't sinking in. When he was about to go, he saw me and took a £10 note out of his pocket.

'There you are, kiddo, buy yourself something nice.'

'No thank you,' I said, turned and walked away.

I hugged Mum for a long time after that. Then she sat at the kitchen table, dinner half-prepared and forgotten. She lit a cigarette. Her hand trembled as she smoked. To see someone so tough – my rock – looking so scared and hurt, was frightening for me. We stayed together, talking and hugging into the night. That bastard had ruined a happy family and, I am sure, had truly broken Mum's heart and shortened her life. She left this earth earlier than she would have done if it weren't for him.

All I could think when I saw the social worker on my doorstep was, 'Who the hell do you think you are?' But by the time we were talking, tea in hand, I thought Mary was all right. It was more like a friendly chat than a Visit with a capital 'V'.

'What help can I offer you?' she said.

'Look, I'm fine. It's been difficult, but I'm getting on top of things again. The kids are happy. We're OK.'

I'd let the wall go up, and I just told Mary what I thought she wanted to hear. As long as she didn't know about the speed and all that came with it, she'd go away and I could carry on as normal. All they thought was that I'd let the house and kids get messy through grief, not through grief combined with drug abuse, which was now coming to dominate my life.

'Tina. You've been through hell and back. I'd understand if you needed help. No one's going to punish you for that, you understand? I'm here to help.'

'I don't need help.'

Mary left. I made promises. I didn't keep them. The kids lived their lives while I watched, like a bystander. I loved them, loved them like any mum would, but I was paralysed into inaction by my mum's death. Something in me had died with her and the speed kept that piece of me that wanted to live down and out.

Then a court summons arrived in the post. I didn't know what it was about. And I really didn't understand when a middle-aged man, Gareth, introduced himself to me outside the court as the appointed guardian for my kids. I was even more confused when I was in the courtroom, my speed still in a wrap in my pocket, when the woman judge started to read out findings from social services. As I listened I knew it was true – the mess, the lack of interaction with my kids who went to school in dirty clothes and exhibited unusual behaviour, crying for no reason, failing to engage with other children. There were so many findings; I wondered how on earth I was going to get out of this.

Then the judge used the words 'neglect' and 'abuse'.

'What the hell is she talking about?' I said, loudly, to anyone and everyone. 'I never hurt my kids. What is she talking about?'

Of course, it being a courtroom, I had to button it or risk being in contempt and finding myself removed, or worse. I assumed they thought I was beating up the kids.

The guardian told me he was going to visit. 'Abuse does not mean you've hit your children,' he said. 'There are many types of abuse and neglect; some more serious than others in the eyes of the court.' He handed me a thin file. 'The judge has told you what you need to do,' he said, tapping it. 'You have to meet this criteria. As long as you work with us and be honest with us then we'll get there.'

I went to the library and found some books about child abuse and soon understood that my children were living in fear and that the risk of them being harmed by my mismanaged existence was real.

First thing to do was to clean the house up but my attempt was half-hearted. More like try and hide the mess, at least the worst of it. I still didn't grasp how serious my situation was. Substance abuse stops you seeing what's right in front of your eyes. There were a number of different social workers who visited and, on the first occasion after the court appearance, it was a tough old boot who came through the door, making me nervous as she paced around the house. She stopped at the kids' bedroom and whisked back the neatly placed duvet. There was no sheet underneath.

'I was getting around to that. Just going to put them in the wash.'

They weren't expecting miracles but the house needed to be adequate at least. As far as cleanliness went, I'd make an effort to clear all the rubbish when I knew social services were about to visit. I did the washing. Sprayed a bit of Febreze, hoovered, skirting the middle. Each time they said they could see I'd made an effort. After they went away, I left it again until the next visit. I didn't see the drugs so much as an issue as a fact of life. They were at the centre of my universe and everything in my life was gradually being pushed away over time. As far as I was concerned, as long as I took them out of sight and never let dealers into the house, then that was OK. No one ever caught me and I never left the drugs lying around or hidden anywhere. They were always kept on me, in my pocket. No one ever knew.

My dad's wife, my step-mum, took her kids to the same school. The teachers mentioned to her that Sophie and Emily were often late and Sophie had come in without any socks on. When the teacher asked Sophie she said, 'Mummy hasn't got any clean ones.'

I was still in touch with Dad. Despite everything, he was my dad and it was a small town, so it was just easier. Dad knew I had problems but was the type to leave me to it. He would say he didn't like to interfere, but this was just another way of saying he was too lazy to bother to help me. My step-mum, Julie, had her head screwed on, though, and was a real fixer. She'd made Dad kick the gambling and get his life back on track. She offered me help, which I refused, but this time the teachers called social services and I was called back to court, where Mary went from being my friend (of course, she'd never been my friend, she'd simply been doing her job) to my enemy as she outlined the case against me. She did try to defend me, talking about all the efforts I'd made at home.

The judge disagreed. 'You have been deceptive and manipulative,' she said, gesturing to a stack of papers – reports about me and my kids. 'You're pretending to work with social services when, in fact, you have no interest in doing so.' I lost the thread after this; what was the point of listening, they'd already made up their minds?

Afterwards, Gareth came to talk to me in the corridor. 'You do understand that this is going to the next level, don't you?'

Taken aback, I asked, 'What's the next level?'

'Your case has been referred to Crown Court, to a bigger, more serious court, where a judge is going to make huge decisions about your life.'

I shrugged. I just didn't get it and I infuriated everyone with my distance, my lack of emotion.

So I went to Crown Court, with my step-mum, and this time there was a stern old male judge in a large, high-ceilinged courtroom with lots of people. The judge talked and talked and I kind of zoned out for a bit until: 'I can come to no other conclusion. The court rules in favour of the children to be removed from the mother's care.'

I looked at my step-mum. 'DO WHAT?' I screamed at the judge, my rantings all being noted by the recorder. When I'd stopped the judge looked me in the eye.

'I understand that you're upset but I must continue with my findings so they are recorded for the court.'

I screamed at him again and again, until nothing was coming out of my mouth, just sobs and gasps. Gareth held me on one side, my step-mum on the other. I looked at Gareth. Right then, if I could, if I'd had the breath in me, I would have killed him.

So history was repeating itself. Mum had lost three kids to the care system. But it had been out of Mum's hands. This was down to me. The social worker came around to see me on the Tuesday and said I'd have the kids until Friday. That was the day they would no longer be mine. 'You have until then to prepare them,' she said. 'To say goodbye.' Did these people actually think this was supposed to make it easier for me? The feeling at this time was unreal, like I was watching it from another world.

I told them on Thursday. 'Tomorrow you're going on an adventure with a friend of mine.'

This was something new and exciting and they were delighted. We packed their bags and in the morning they were hopping up and down, waiting for my friend to come and take them on an adventure.

'Is this your friend, Mum?' asked Sophie.

'Yes, yes, that's her.'

I had booster seats for them and sat them in the back of the car, helped them with seat belts, put the bags into the boot and waved them off, smiling to the last. The moment I stepped back into my house, a shell without my children, I wanted to smash the place up, burn it down; then I wanted to smash myself up. But my energy, what little there was of it, vanished and I fell to my knees and stretched out in the hallway. At some point I went upstairs and lay across the girls' beds and the next thing I knew a week had gone by. At some point I took an overdose. I didn't even know what it was I took, just every pill I could find. I woke up after being out for I don't know how long. My head, fuzzy, was banging, and my pillow had become stuck to my face with thick drool. 'I can't even kill myself,' I thought. 'Can't even do that right. And now I've got the mother of all headaches and I've taken all the pills in the house.'

I went to the kitchen and ate a packet of biscuits, one after the other. Gareth had told me on the day of the court case: 'We can turn this around. You're articulate. You're not stupid. Right now you can't see the wood for the trees.'

I didn't think I could. My girls had been removed. People, my family, were all going to judge me. They would think I'd done terrible things to the children I loved, really loved with all my heart. If I had them now, I thought, I would take better care of them; I'd show them all. But then reality sunk in. That wasn't going to happen. As long as I was taking drugs, my chances would be non-existent.

As my headache started to fade, I looked in my pocket for the speed. It was there, as it always was. The doorbell went. It was Mary. She at least knew not to ask me how I was doing or tell me I looked like shit. And now, I just couldn't be bothered to hide my drug use. I opened the wrap, wet my finger and dabbed it into the white crystals.

'What's that?'

'Amphetamine. You know, speed.'

Mary looked like the mother of all pennies had dropped. 'But you're such an articulate young lady – we never even guessed. How long?'

I shrugged. 'Since I don't know when.'

ANGELIKA

Angelika was a young care leaver who had read Hackney Child *and I had become her mentor. We bonded automatically, before understanding why. I think now that we could each see something of ourselves in the other and, as Angelika told her story, I saw parallels, particularly emotional parallels that came through love lost as a child and the subsequent search for love that followed – with all the danger that entails.*

I was born in a small town in Poland. Our family life was good, until Mum and Dad really started to argue when I was nine years old. They tried to keep it from me, but children are sensitive and I can still feel the bad atmosphere that filled the house. I had a sister, Davina, who was four years younger than me, and a brother, Stanislaw (we called him Stan or Stanny), who was seven years younger than me. Dad was tall, dark-haired, handsome and tough. He'd been in the army and worked as a security guard. Mum was a chef, a really great cook and was small, blonde and extremely pretty. I wanted to be just like her when I grew up.

Mum and Dad divorced when I was ten. Dad was working but money was tight and he decided to go to England where he could earn a lot more and send it home to us.

'We'll get rich and fat,' he joked, tickling me, 'and I'll build you your very own fairy palace.'

But when Dad went away, we didn't hear from him. I was really upset about that.

My mum quickly found a new boyfriend, Patek. He was tall, blond and full of muscles. He was also vain and violent and I hated him so much. When Mum was at the restaurant, he would drink from a tin until he wobbled when he stood up and then he'd beat up four-year-old Stanny. I mean he didn't smack, he really hit him with his closed fist. He thought that was how you taught young boys to be men. I was scared for a few days before I decided to tell Mum and she kicked Patek out straight away. Then there was another boyfriend, Gregory, an older man with huge, scarred hands, a shiny, bald head and a big, hard stomach. We all lived together in a little bungalow and every night I wished Dad was with us.

He'd been gone nearly two years.

When Gregory lived with us, us kids slept in one large room and Mum and Gregory slept in the lounge. One time I woke up at night to go to the toilet and I heard a lot of people in the lounge, talking and laughing. I peeked in. The room was lit by candles and there were lots of men smoking and drinking. They didn't notice me as I walked into the foggy room. I could see Mum in bed with the covers all pulled up, so I went over to ask her what was going on. I pulled off the covers and saw another man – not Gregory – lying there with her. I started crying. Stanny and Davina woke up and came into the room. Mum lied, saying I wasn't feeling well and they should go back to bed. I felt really awful about the lie. I wanted to say so but I knew Mum would be cross if I didn't, so I just kept quiet.

When I was twelve years old, playing with Stanny in the garden, Mum came out holding the telephone. 'It's Dad,' she said. 'He's coming home.'

I was so happy he was coming back. I'd missed him so much but was still angry with him for leaving us for so long. I was also angry with Mum for living with all these strange and horrible men.

Every now and again, since Dad had gone, Mum would give us chocolates and biscuits that came in packets with foreign writing on them. She never said where they came from but I just assumed, like a lot of things she bought, that she got them cheap from someone on the black market. When Dad arrived, the first thing I noticed was that he'd brought a big suitcase full of presents, including these sweets. Then it clicked. He'd been sending us presents all the time!

I asked him about it and he said: 'Didn't you get my letters?' He'd been writing to us as well and Mum had hidden the letters. I was so happy. Dad still loved us, he'd missed us and now he wanted us all to go to England. I hated Mum at first for what she'd done but Dad said: 'You mustn't blame your mama. It was difficult for her when I left. Things are going to be better now, I promise.'

And he was right. Mum and Dad got back together and we were a normal family again for almost two years. Dad would go back to London, which I got very anxious about, but this time they were much shorter visits, a month at a time. One day he came back all excited and announced that he and Mum had decided to move to the UK – schools, a house, a job had all been arranged. We were going to live in Barnet near London, in a lovely large house on the edge of a wood, not far from our school. The plan involved sharing the house with another family that Dad knew from Poland. They had two kids aged fifteen and seven.

It was exciting but confusing being in another country. I couldn't speak English and it was difficult at school for the first three months, while I desperately tried to work out what the other thirteen-year-olds were talking about. I'm sure they were sometimes saying nasty things about me but, once I could join in, I made some friends.

I also saw a black person for the first time when Mum and I were walking down the high street. I was so shocked that I couldn't help myself and asked: 'Why is he so dirty?' She was so shocked and angry that she slapped me. Dad was working the nightshift at a steady job and, while we weren't rich, we had enough. We were living a normal, easy life – a normal, little family.

After a year, when I was fifteen years old, we moved into a house of our own. Mum and Dad started to argue again. I was playing with Davina in the front garden when Mum suddenly burst out of the house and stomped down the garden path, her large handbag stuffed full and tucked under her arm.

'Mum? Where are you going?'

'To see a friend around the corner. I won't be long.' She marched off down the street without looking back.

'Another row with Dad,' I thought and forgot about it. But she didn't come back that night, or the next night, so Dad reported Mum missing to the police. Then he noticed his credit card was gone. One night became three nights and then a week, then two weeks. Dad checked with the bank and found that someone had spent £2,000 on his credit card. Dad spent a lot of time looking for Mum and at first his boss was sympathetic and gave him time off but then, as Dad missed more days and refused to work nights because he didn't feel comfortable leaving us home alone at night, he was fired. It turned out that the family finances were on a knife-edge and by the time Dad had paid the monthly bills, we were suddenly in debt without even the credit card to turn to. We lived off the cheapest food and Dad had to ask friends for £30 to tide us over until Mum came back and he could find another job. If it hadn't been for these friends, we would have starved.

Three weeks later, Mum suddenly reappeared with no explanation and acted like everything was fine. She knew we were worried, that the police were looking for her, but she wouldn't explain. I was just glad that everything had returned to normal, although I was a bit anxious that it might happen again.

One month later, I came home from school to find my room had been ransacked. Burglars had taken everything, including – most painfully of all – a white gold necklace my dad had bought for me for my thirteenth birthday, which was worth about £400, along with all my other little pieces of jewellery, which couldn't have been worth much. I ran to Dad screaming that we'd been robbed.

'No, we haven't,' he replied. It was true – the rest of the

house was fine. Eventually we had to accept that it was Mum. She had taken everything I owned that was saleable. I didn't understand it. How could my mum have done this to me? Didn't she love me? Had she never loved me?

Dad reported her missing again. When Mum came back, two weeks later, she'd even sold her wedding ring. Still she wouldn't explain. Dad was at a loss but felt he had to take Mum back so he could go to work while she looked after us kids.

The next time she left, she vanished for three weeks with Dad's pay packet.

She came back one night when we were eating cheap boiled pasta with tasteless tomato ketchup. Dad had changed the locks. After she started to kick the door, Dad put down his fork and told us to finish our dinner. We got up and watched from the kitchen doorway as Dad opened the front door. Mum went to step in. Dad stopped her.

'You do not live here any more and we do not need you any more,' he said. 'We no longer care about you. Just go away and do whatever you're doing.'

He closed the door. Mum wouldn't go, however, and screamed at Dad through the letterbox. Stanny and Davina were really scared, so Dad called the police. They already knew about our troubles with Mum because of all the times Dad had reported her missing. They arrested Mum and banned her from coming anywhere near our house.

So much for a better life in England. Stanny, who was now nine years old, and Davina, who was twelve, both struggled at school after Mum left. I did OK, but I didn't understand what had happened to Mum and couldn't make my brother and sister feel any better, and neither could Dad.

Stanny was angry with Dad for not making Mum stay, and his pain and frustration came out at school. He argued with his teachers, was disruptive in class and fell in with the 'bad kids', kids like him who came from unstable and unhappy homes.

Stanny started to steal to impress his new friends – from shops, from school and from other children. I think he really needed the love of a mother. Dad really tried but he was unused to being a stay-at-home parent and he had been left just as confused and upset by Mum's behaviour as we had.

Mum vanished for a couple of months and then she got in touch with Dad, asking to come back. Dad resisted but could see his family falling apart in front of him. He'd found part-time work for when we were at school. He needed work to make some money so we could live better, but we also needed our mum's love, no matter how messed up she was. We needed something she had that Dad couldn't provide and, whatever it was, it was really important.

Dad let her into the house for a short visit about five months after the police arrested her. It was getting close to Christmas and I asked Dad if she could come for Christmas dinner, to help me cook as I didn't know how. He agreed. Polish Christmas dinner is very different from an English one and it involves twelve traditional courses, all of which have to be prepared from scratch, including red borscht, mushroom soup, carp, herrings and dumplings stuffed with cabbage, sauerkraut or mushrooms, as well as cabbage rolls and gingerbread and poppy seed cake for dessert. Dad made enough money that Christmas to get all of these things and more, and so he put food on the table and Mum cooked it. It felt like we were a family again.

I was so proud of my dad because he kept everything together for us, had worked so hard and was still trying to find a way to get Mum permanently back in our lives. I think he loved her, despite her craziness. But, more than that, he could see how much we needed her.

The next secret was revealed when Mum couldn't hide it any more. She was pregnant. And not by our dad.

I came home from school one day to find a man and a woman from social services waiting to talk to me. They asked me lots of questions about home, school, and my mum and dad, until I got fed up and ran to find Dad: 'Why all the personal questions? What's happened?'

'They say I beat up your brother,' he answered.

'But that's ridiculous!' I shouted, running back to the social worker. 'Dad never hit Stanny! Dad loves him; he loves us all. He wouldn't harm any of us. He's only ever cared for us.'

After Mum had revealed she was pregnant, Stanny got into more and more trouble at school until he picked on kids much bigger than him and they beat him up. He'd asked me for help – he always did – and he told the other kids: 'My sister's here now and she's going to fight all of you.'

I was tired of always having to defend him, to justify him to teachers and other kids, and so this time I said: 'No, I'm not. You have to fight your own battles. It's your mess. You made it, you sort it out.'

When the teacher saw the results of Stanny's one-sided fight, instead of telling on the other children, he said the bruises had come from Dad. Stanny didn't come home that night.

Dad sat up until the next morning. I found him in the kitchen. His skin looked grey and, for the first time, in that weak morning light, I saw my dad as an old man.

'Why would Stanny say something like that?' he asked.

'Because he wants the attention,' I said. 'And because he can't admit he lied, that he was wrong to lie.'

Social services said that Stanny wouldn't be coming home for a while and he was placed with foster carers. It didn't take long, however, before his foster carers were bringing Stanny to the house for a few hours every other day. The first time, they dropped him off, Dad hugged Stanny so hard and for so long I thought he was going to hurt him. Dad didn't ask Stanny why he'd done what he had. They both knew and understood what had happened and why and what the situation was. Between them, they said and did everything social services needed to hear so that Stanny could come home and live with us again. But the process was really slow. There were assessments, ones that had to be booked months in advance, and surprise visits that could take place at any day and at any time social services cared to choose. We understood the purpose but it was really hard to live through it. Mum was there with us but not really present. She was pregnant with this other man's child and she seemed to be half-in and half-out of our lives. It took four months but finally Stanny was allowed home. And he almost immediately started getting in trouble again.

I'd been saving up, using all my spare change, and had about £40 in a jar in my room when it went missing. I asked

Davina what had happened and she started to cry, confessing that Stanny had given her £5 not to say anything.

I got hold of Stanny and told him to give me the money.

'I don't have it.'

'Give it back to me.'

I grabbed him, shaking him, not noticing he had a knife in his hand. 'What are you doing?'

He screamed, 'Go away, go away, go away!' and as he struggled to push me away, he somehow swiped the blade between my thumb and forefinger, managing to slice out a good piece of flesh. The doctor stitching me up asked me how I did it. I said I cut it on a can. He paused and looked up for a moment, caught my eye, knew I was lying and carried on. Neither of us said anything more as he finished the stitches.

By this time I was headed down a bad route. I'd started smoking cigarettes before quickly moving on to cannabis, spending all I could on this wonderful natural herb that made me feel so good. If it was a dark December day, raining and cold, smoking cannabis made it seem as though the sun was shining in a city of rainbows. When Dad found out, he got really cross. He put all drugs in the same class – grass was as bad as heroin, as far as he was concerned and, even though he demanded and then begged me to stop, I refused. Eventually, when neither of us would back down, I left home.

To begin with I stayed with friends and managed to live for six weeks this way, hiding in bedrooms and spare rooms. I didn't like living off their charity, so looked for something to do to make money. Which was harder than I first thought. I was at a friend's house, bored, while she was out trying to buy some grass, when I met her older sister, a glamorous eighteen-year-old called Kath. Her room smelled like a shop – that smell of new stuff – and it was full of boxes. There were designer clothes, electronic gizmos of every description – from men's shavers to laptops – and a few bottles of perfume, all in their original boxes.

'What's all this?' I asked. 'Where'd you get all this cool stuff?'

'Don't touch none of it,' she said. 'I've got to take it back later to get refunds.'

She told me how she worked with a gang doing something called bar code fraud. This is when you go to Boots or John Lewis, for example, and pick out the most expensive DVD player, priced at £500, and swap its bar code for the cheapest one, say £50. She would then pay for it with cash. Later she would go back and get a refund, also always in cash (you don't need a receipt to get a refund, according to UK law). If they wouldn't give her a cash refund, she'd say that she'd decided to keep the item, and then give it to her boss who had people he could sell it to. Sometimes he would give her bar codes to stick over the original ones.

'I could do that!' I said.

'You're too young.'

'I'm sixteen,' I said (I was actually fifteen). 'And when I dress up I look a lot older.' I kept on at Kath until she agreed to introduce me to her boss, who turned out to be a chubby, middle-aged white man from Manchester who wore tight T-shirts and dirty, grey tracksuit bottoms. He employed thirty women working from ten cars in seven-day shifts all around the UK. He paid all my expenses

– travel, cheap hotels and food – so all my basic living needs were taken care of. Anything I made I could spend on what I liked – drugs, booze and clothes. I started slowly and made about £30 each day after exchanging several thousand pounds' worth of gear. It was a massive operation and must have come to over a million pounds in terms of the amount of goods stolen and money exchanged over a year or two.

The driver of the car, usually a woman in her early twenties, was in charge and if we got caught we had to say that she was our guardian, which meant she was allowed to pick us up from the police station. I think I stayed in every single Travelodge in the UK. My boss and colleagues didn't care that I was fifteen and officially missing from home; after all, this was a criminal enterprise. All that counted was my ability to change tags and buy and return goods according to their instructions.

I bought a mobile phone to stay in touch with Stanny and Davina and, after two weeks on the road, I got a call from Stanny's social worker. She said that Stanny hadn't stopped fighting and the situation had worsened to the extent that several older boys were out to get him and had thrown a brick through our lounge window. It was too dangerous to leave Stanny and Davina in the house, so they were going to take them into care.

All I could think about was how mad and upset Dad was going to be when he found out. Mum didn't seem to care about anyone or anything these days. I was in John Lewis when I got the call. I took a bar code glued on to a cheap men's shaver and stuck it on to the most expensive model worth almost £300. It was all going fine, as it normally did, until I got to the checkout and the bloke saw both bar codes. I'd forgotten to remove the original.

After a quick review of the CCTV footage, I was arrested. My boss got me out, as promised, but I got caught again almost the next day, this time in Leeds. I didn't want to end up in court, so I said I wanted to leave. 'No one's stopping you,' my boss said, so I took off, there and then.

We were in Manchester and for some reason I decided to do a bit of shoplifting on my own. I still don't know why I thought this was such a good idea. I was caught for the third time in a matter of days. The police were really nice to me; they didn't charge me and even put me on a train back to London when I told them I just wanted to go home. They probably should have called my dad, but it felt to me as if this was the quickest, easiest option for them and that was fine with me. Instead of going home when I arrived in London, I met up with a friend and carried on. The next time I was caught shoplifting, a social worker appeared.

She was really nice and explained that she wanted to help me sort things out for my family and the best thing I could do would be to go into foster care before anything too disastrous happened to me. She explained that a gang had attacked our house again, this time smashing every single window in the house. I couldn't go home and I was obviously rubbish at shoplifting. Maybe foster care wasn't such a bad idea.

SARAH

Sarah came into my life like a beautiful gift. I had been in recovery from my own addiction for three and a half years and was feeling a bit bored of the same people being in the same recovery meetings. Sarah appeared shy, looked vulnerable in a wistful way, and far younger than her years. The connection felt instant, even before I realised the crucial lessons that she would teach me over the coming years – lessons about the reality of what it is like to have a baby, carried inside you for nine months, taken away because of your addiction. The battle to refuse to remain in that place, to refuse to allow the trauma to trap you into more pregnancies, resulting in the same outcome. I had no idea what it felt like for my own mum to have that first baby so cruelly taken. I felt such love and pain for my mum over the coming months as I got to know Sarah, grieving for the loss of my sister, and grieving for my mum and the loss she suffered at not being able to be a mum to my sister, and not being able to make the remarkable changes that Sarah somehow found the strength to make.

I don't remember life with my birth mother. Dad worked while Mum stayed at home with me and my older brother and sister. The neighbour would babysit while Mum did her make-up and went out for the night. She was beautiful and found it impossible to stop having affairs and so Dad, fed up beyond forgiveness, eventually decided to end it. Us kids stayed with Dad while Mum moved in with one of her short-term lovers.

My first memory is of my fourth birthday, of my dad and step-mum laughing at the tacky, pound-shop make-up Mum had sent me. Dad used to say I looked just like her, but I can't say I've ever seen it myself. I could barely see her past all the bright colours, make-up and jewellery she liked to wear.

My sister, brother and I reluctantly went to visit Mum every now and again. She once yelled at us, 'Why do you come and see me if you hate it so much?'

My brother answered, 'Because Dad wants us to.'

She slapped me once, after I called her a 'megabitch' for leaving Dad and generally being a pain.

We carried on like this until I was six, at which point Mum just vanished. She didn't explain and I blamed myself. The pain of the abandonment stayed with me – although for many years afterwards I did not realise where it came from.

Life at home was good, although Dad smoked a lot of weed and drank quite a bit (but not as much as Mum had). He was a good father to us and our step-mum was lovely. Dad was strict and protective and trouble came after I turned twelve. I started wanting to go out but Dad forbade me to go beyond our local park. I obeyed until, goaded by friends, I decided to ignore him. The problem was, because I was frightened of him, I delayed coming home because I knew he'd be angry with me and so I stayed out later and later until it was dawn the following morning. I'd started the evening hanging out with friends, then went to a party and from there we went to another party, which turned out to be at a squat, full of drunk and drugged-up eighteen-year-old kids and a few crackheads.

I was still there the next day when a woman came up to me with a piece of paper. 'You have to go home,' she said. She handed me the paper. It was a bad photocopy of my passport photo. 'Found it tacked to a lamp post,' she said.

That left me even more scared but I think she must have called the number because a short time later Dad kicked the front door off its hinges and dragged me out.

Instead of being mad, however, Dad was just happy I was safe and I got lots of attention, kisses and cuddles. This I really liked; Dad had stopped kissing and cuddling me since he'd said I was becoming 'a young lady'. I thought if cuddles were going to happen every time I went missing, then I'd go missing again. These signs of affection quickly wore off and eventually turned to anger and frustration, by which time I'd been hooked into hanging out with the wrong crowd, and I'd stopped caring about school. Dad decided to send me to live with Mum to get me away from my 'bad' friends, but I just used her flat as a hotel and hardly spoke to her – only asking for money and, when she said no, taking it from her purse. She couldn't cope either and so, after asking for help from the council, I was given a room in a hostel for the homeless. I was seventeen years old. Everyone else there was in their thirties and forties and they all, without exception, spent the day getting smashed any which way they could. I loved it. It was like one long party and I'd hang out with them and visit the squat they bought their drugs from, a large house in Finsbury Park in north London, which smelled funny but the party never stopped. People were always smoking, drinking and listening to music. We ate for free from the Hare Krishna food van and from a home-less charity that gave us a delicious meat stew and cheese rolls from a once-weekly soup kitchen in Arlington Road, near Camden Market.

I was in another squat, quite a nice one, it was clean and tidy compared to the others I'd seen, and I was high, as usual, when this ferocious-looking old man came in and frightened me by speaking in an incomprehensible growl. At that moment another man appeared from another door, older, good-looking and when he spoke, he sounded just like Dad, so I ran over to him and hugged him, asking: 'Can I hang out with you?'

The man's name was Robbie and he said of course and we took speed together. Later on, I watched him injecting heroin.

'Can I try it?'

Robbie did it for me and I loved it straight away. The feeling was like a constant gentle soaring, a lovely, warm, out-of-body experience – like having an extremely long cuddle. Robbie took care of everything, of getting the drugs and looking after me and he would go and do what-ever he had to do to raise the money, which usually involved stealing copper. Once we were evicted from that squat, we found another one that was a lot more unpleasant. It was filthy and freezing – there were no windows, no electric and no gas. Thank God the water was working. I didn't like it at all but I didn't consider going home, I just wanted lots of warm hugs from those delicious injections.

I woke up one morning to find a policeman with a disgusted expression on his face standing in my room. He told me to get up. I'd breached a community order I'd received for being drunk and disorderly some time earlier by not checking in at the police station. There were more officers downstairs arresting Robbie because the house was full of stolen copper piping that he was selling to support us. The police officer couldn't believe it when I told him Robbie was my boyfriend. 'He's in his forties! He's over twenty years older than you.'

I just shrugged.

He got bail but I was given a prison sentence of sixty days. It started to sink in when I was on my way to Holloway and I cried my eyes out. I'd been fainting and suffering dizzy spells (Robbie said it was lack of food because I wasn't eating properly) and could barely walk from the prison van to the 'check-in' area. Part of the routine of checking in involved a medical, after which I was told: 'You're pregnant.'

The prison officers were quite sympathetic to me after that, even agreeing to let me have a single cell, after I begged to be alone. I was soon moved, however, for lack of space, and then I was in a cell with four drug addicts who were all taking heroin in the toilets. It seemed as though getting drugs in prison was just as easy as it was on the outside. Maybe it was thanks to the pregnancy, but I had no trouble staying off drugs and, after two months, I went home clean. Home this time was to Dad, who immediately told me there was nothing for him to forgive and he took me back in.

But I was in love with Robbie and I fully expected him to look after me and our baby. He was still using and when he asked if I'd like to have some heroin, I agreed. It never even occurred to me to think of the health of the baby until I went to the hospital for a check-up.

'Take a seat,' the nurse said. 'We need to take some blood for testing, I'll just get set up and then I'll call you in, OK?'

I nodded and, as soon as her back was turned, I snuck out.

I couldn't stay at home if I wanted to keep taking drugs and, as the council told me they wouldn't house me until I'd given birth, Robbie said I could stay in his ex-girlfriend's spare room. I should have thought this was a bit weird, but my head was all over the place and I didn't give it a thought. I barely slept or ate, I just listened to music and made sure I stayed as high as possible, for as long as possible, until I passed out. Robbie never let me down and always seemed able to bring something back for me. I was also on probation and was supposed to be checking in with them, but I decided, for obvious reasons, that I wasn't going to have any more contact with anyone official.

I was waiting anxiously for Robbie when the labour pains started. I'd been using constantly, had barely slept for two weeks and was feeling really edgy when a cramp caused me to gasp in surprise.

By the time Robbie turned up, I was doubled over in

pain. We went to the hospital. The doctor said I was still at least three days from giving birth and Robbie wanted me to go home so, as always, I did what he wanted. He was as much of a drug as the heroin.

I was woken by a smashing sound and, once again, I opened my eyes to find a police officer in the room.

'We're looking for Robbie,' he said. 'Where is he?'

I was covered with blankets and wrapped up in coats and jumpers and he didn't realise I was pregnant.

'I've no idea,' I said. 'Haven't seen him in ages.'

They could see I was high and not much use as an interview subject and they left. The next time I awoke, Robbie was on the bed, shaking me awake.

'I think I can see the baby's head,' he said.

I was ambulanced to hospital and was put into a specialist unit where I immediately gave birth. The nurse let me see and touch him for a moment; he was crying but so small. At two kilos he was really underweight and I only saw him for a few seconds before they took him into intensive care – the memory is a blur.

I said I wasn't using when the nurse asked but she just nodded down at the old and new needle marks scarring my forearms. She didn't need to ask, no one did. Michael, my baby, did well; he was soon out of intensive care.

The nurses said I could breastfeed Michael and he just latched on.

'Aw, you'll make an excellent mum,' one of the nurses told me.

A young social services lady turned up and spoke to the nurses. They kept me in the special care unit and then the recovery unit for ten days – which sobered me up – before I found out what was going on. They were going to take my baby. I got up and demanded we both be discharged but the nurses stalled me until the police arrived with an emergency court order that allowed them to take Michael into 72-hour police protection. He was moved away from me to another hospital.

At every stage, I didn't know what was going to happen. Everything was an unpleasant shock. I'm sure people had tried to tell me what was about to take place but it wasn't until the heroin left my body that I regained my senses. It was only when I started to attend the daily supervised visits to see my son that I began to understand that he wasn't coming home with me, that there was something wrong with the way I was living.

Looking at my tiny son nestled up against me, I decided I didn't want to use any more. I still loved Robbie, however, and there was no way he was going to stop using.

Michael was taken into foster care and was placed with an elderly couple who lived near my dad, which was great as it meant I could see him every day. Robbie was forbidden from seeing his son and he wasn't happy about that at all. He didn't see how his heroin addiction came into it.

'None of my other kids have been taken into care,' he moaned and, while this was true – he had three children with two other women – they weren't in care because he hardly had any contact with any of them and the mothers were doing great jobs of raising them entirely on their own.

My social worker seemed really young to me and I didn't trust her. I spotted a torn packet of King Size Rizlas in her car, so I was certain she was smoking weed and that made me think, 'Who is she to tell me what I'm doing is wrong when she's a drug user, too?'

'Michael was removed from your care because of your drug use and your relationship with Robbie,' she told me. 'You can't be with Robbie if you want to be a mother to Michael. That's never going to work.'

I was puzzled. How did they know what Robbie was like? I had no idea they'd spoken to him. I was also really surprised that I was seen as a risk to Michael. I had no idea, they didn't tell me at any time that they were doing an assessment and what their analysis of me might mean.

'So what's next?' I asked.

'If you accept a mother and baby placement with a foster family who will supervise you, then you can move in with them with Michael. You'll stay there for a few months and then a decision can be made as to your future.'

I agreed and moved with Michael to a house a long way from home – in a small town by the sea on the south coast. At first I was devastated and couldn't understand why Robbie couldn't come. Despite what I'd been told, I still thought that we could be a family.

The foster mum, Maggie, reminded me of my step-mum. She was amazing, so chatty but in a way that made me feel really relaxed, like I was a member of the family from the first moment. I was appalling at social interaction – I'd spent the last two years in bed floating on a heroin cloud. On top of this, I was scared about the placement, but Maggie did her best to put me at ease.

'Here I am rabbiting on, you must be exhausted,' she said, beaming at me. 'You get unpacked, come back down and we'll have a cup of tea and a piece of cake waiting for you.'

My room was beautiful. I could hear the sea washing over pebbles and, carrying Michael, I walked over to the window. There was even a balcony. I stood on it and watched the waves for a while and forgot all about unpacking. I felt like I'd been given a second chance, I could start again clean, and I was determined not to let Michael down.

Maggie and her husband, Dave, had two beautiful daughters. Dave would joke that we ladies were ganging up on him, as we always outnumbered him in family votes. And that was how they made me feel – like part of the family. They showed me so much care and love and they let me get on with being a mum. They didn't interfere or push me down any particular route; they just let me find my way with Michael.

They wanted me to carry on living there but, as much as I liked it, I still missed Robbie, the man I loved.

'Wouldn't you want to go back to Dave, if you were forced to be apart like me?' I asked Maggie.

'Yes, but Dave isn't taking drugs, Sarah, and I don't have a little baby.'

Although Michael had been born small, he'd made an amazing recovery. It seemed that despite my drug use, I'd been blessed with a beautiful, perfect little boy. And I did as much as I could to make it up to him as a mother. I was supposed to be writing daily reports for social services, but after a couple of weeks they reduced them to weeklies as I was doing so well.

After five months at Maggie and Dave's, social services gave me the all clear.

I could not have done it without Maggie, Dave and their family.

I asked Robbie, 'Would you give it up for me and for your son? So we can be a family?'

He looked at me a long while. I loved his eyes; they were the nicest thing about him. Despite the drug abuse, they were clear blue and sparkled no matter how dull the light was.

'Yes,' he said, stroking my face, 'I would do that for you.'

PETE

Pete and I had been friends ever since living in the same chil-dren's home as kids. He was a mixed-up kid, joking one moment, bullying the next. He did not know when he was crossing inap-propriate lines, something that hadn't been solved by the time he left the home. Out in the 'real world', Pete became a danger to society and himself. His story serves both as a terrible warning and, I hope, an inspiration that the capacity for positive change lies in everyone – without exception.

I was having the Addict Dream again. Night-time. Of course. I'm in a squat. Naturally. A lounge. Dark carpets and ratty furniture. The smell of dampness and cold. All is as it should be.

Except for the fact that in front of me is a roll of tin foil, a bank note, a mirror, cigarettes, a plastic bank card, a lighter, a brown lump of sticky hashish, a small plastic bag filled with white crystalline powder that I know is speed and another bag that contains heroin. I am surrounded by dozens of cans of high-strength, ice-cold beer. I don't know where to start. I'm on my own. Everything is mine. I don't know what I've done to deserve this good fortune but something inside me tells me I have no time to waste, so I get started. I roll a joint, a large one with three King Size Rizlas, line it with tobacco, burn and crumble the hashish, pop in a roach made from the card of the Rizla packet, roll it, lick and stick, twist the end and tap it down. I fire it up and draw in the smoke with hungry sucking breaths. It burns and I feel my saliva production go into overdrive. I suck again, holding my breath, and I lay the joint on the table, while I reach for the speed, cut a fat line on the mirror, roll the note and snort. My nose explodes, my brain lights up electric blue and turns to ice as I swallow and the thick, sticky amphetamines pulse down the back of my throat and this sets my mind on cold fire with the thought of the rush yet to come. Then it is there and my head glows more and more brightly until it explodes with orgasmic pleasure, oh please, please, please, please, never let it stop, and I'm riding a wave of pure rushing and soaring joy until I feel as though I can't take any more. But I want it to take me past what's possible, so that it kills me and, as I hover over that ultimate moment, the wave crashes, and I'm left with a terrible feeling of uncertainty, anxiety and a plunging, lead-weight-to-the-bottom-of-the-river sensation of fear. Desperately, I reach for the heroin and place a fat line of the brownish powder on the foil, shiny side down, and hold the rolled note in my mouth. As I burn the foil's underside, the heroin liquefies and evaporates and I draw it in. The taste is metallic and flowery and I wait for the hit, the joy of pain gone, of relief, that the thing that spends every moment of my life eating me up inside vanishes. It almost but doesn't quite go away. My head is pulsing, I can hardly breathe from everything I've just inhaled but it's not enough. I grab the joint and take another draw. Then another, and another line of speed, and another. I pour all of the heroin into the foil and burn it, sucking, sucking until I can't feel my mouth and my lungs are raw. I open a beer and pour it in and my tongue comes back to life, tasting of something rancid, of rotten oranges. I can't feel my throat as I swallow and I choke. I smoke more, more, more. I drink and my head is full of the taste of a high but none of the high itself. I look at the table and there's a mess of powder and paraphernalia and I can't see any more drugs. Nothing left. And I start to search. I wet my finger to collect powder, I lick the mirror, unravel and lick the note and shake, panic, scream that I want to die, die, die . . .

I wake, swearing and sweating. I don't know where I am for a moment and then I remember. My drug taking is all behind me. My heart breaks at the thought as it always does, that I won't be able to have another hit, never, ever again in my life. I think about killing myself, as I always do. I could do it, of course. But if I do then everything will be lost. I gave up so much to get here. Fought so hard. For what, I'm still not sure, except that it can't be for nothing. And then I remember.

I'd run away from more children's homes than I had fingers and toes. Every time I ran away they put me in another one.

Every time I think of the children's homes, I am reminded of why I was there.

A police interview room. I was seven years old. One of my first clear memories. The cops were really nice to me (not so much once I grew up, when I was six feet tall and found out I was able to hurt them). They talked to me about school (which I liked; I was especially interested in dinosaurs and outer space), as well as my friends (I didn't have many; I wasn't exactly popular and I didn't really know what to say to anyone) and games (kicking a ball against a wall on my own). It was cosy. Not like how I imagined a police interview to be from the telly and the way my dad and everyone at school spoke about them. They hated the cops.

I was interviewed by a woman. There was a man there, older, like a granddad. I didn't have a granddad.

'You live in a flat in Somers Town with your mum and dad, don't you, Pete?'

'Yes.'

'Any brothers or sisters?'

'No.'

'What does your dad do?'

'Nothing.'

'He doesn't have a job?'

'No, he can't work 'cause he's sick.'

'Does your dad sometimes shout when he's at home?'

'Yes.'

'How does that make you feel, when he shouts?'

'Scared.'

'What do you do when he shouts?'

'I put my hands over my ears and shut my eyes.'

'Does your dad shout at your mummy sometimes?'

'All the time. She screams at him sometimes.'

'Does he shout at you?'

'Yes. When he drinks a lot.'

'How often does he drink?'

'Every day.'

'Does he frighten you when he's drinking?'

'Yes.'

'Does he frighten you when he's not drunk?'

'I don't know.'

'You don't know if he frightens you?'

'I don't know when he's not drunk.'

'Do you go out together as a family?'

'No.'

'Do you play together?'

'No.'

'Does your dad ever hit you?'

This one was hard. Dad did hit me but I kind of knew that if I said he did then he'd be in a lot of trouble. That might mean he'd hit me again when I got home. I felt like I was already in trouble. The police had turned up when Mum and Dad's screams led to a window being smashed with a brick. I don't know where it had come from but it had somehow ended up landing on someone's car.

'That's all right, Peter; you don't have to answer if you don't want to.'

Cool. I nodded and waited. I'd think about that one for a bit longer. I liked the woman who was interviewing me. She had a nice voice. I don't think Dad would have ever tried to hit her.

'Does your dad ever hit your mum?'

Now I was on safer ground. Everyone knew that, right? The police had even been around before and seen it for themselves.

'A lot. Dad hits Mum a lot.'

What I didn't know was that this time Dad had hit Mum so hard he broke her jaw, putting her in a coma.

'You're doing great,' the woman said.

I nodded. Sure I was.

'Did your mum ever try and stop your dad from hitting her?'

'She can't. She wants to but he's way too strong.'

'And what happened last night?'

I stayed quiet.

'Peter? Can you tell me what happened?'

Silence.

'It's OK, you don't have to but it would be helpful if you could tell us a little bit about what happened.'

Dad would do many unpleasant things to me. For no reason at all. I'd be walking across the lounge, he'd be sitting on the sofa, drinking, watching something on the box and before I knew what was going on, my head was ringing from a punch that had left me on the floor.

That was nothing, though. I got used to getting hit. That stood me in good stead later on. The other stuff he did was harder to deal with. He rubbed curry powder in my eyes. He burned me with hot water. He choked me until my eyes started to roll back into my head. He held my head down the toilet. All the time he told me what a worthless little piece of rubbish I was. There was never any reason, any explanation for why I was this little piece of rubbish. That was what I was and that was all there was to say. Mum was usually asleep or being hit by Dad, too. I wasn't going to tell the cops this, though.

No one had loved me. I hadn't loved anyone. Didn't know how, or what it was. Didn't think I ever would. I never loved or cried or felt happy. Only for moments at a time. And when I laughed it was cruel – because I was about to do something bad, or had just done something bad.

I never told the police what really happened that night. What Dad had done. I couldn't. The words wouldn't come.

I never knew my dad, not really. He was just a tightly wound, wiry ball of fury who was angry with everyone, all of the time. Especially me and Mum.

Mum had a problem I never knew about. She'd managed to keep her benzodiazepine habit from me. It was odd because afterwards, when someone finally explained it to me and I understood, I knew. I knew she was keeping something from me. I knew there was a secret, that something wasn't right. The feeling was so strong I never doubted it for a moment and I think that the social worker who told me was expecting a much bigger reaction. But I displayed what a psychiatrist later described as 'flat affect'. Zero emotion.

It made total sense to me – why mum was always tired and forgetting stuff that made Dad angry and beat her up. She needed relief from the stress of living with Dad. Me and her both.

Anyway, with Dad looking at jail time and Mum unable or unwilling to stop taking her pills, I was fostered for a while but I proved 'difficult' and was put in a home for 'special' children, which only increased my tendency towards violence. I ran away as soon as I could. I was moved to other children's homes and when I was sixteen they stopped worrying about me when I ran away. There was a routine. I'd leave, they'd report it and I'd come back, but in my own time. It worked just fine.

The first time I took drugs suddenly all the shit that clogged up my mind every day wasn't there any more. I had no fear of any drug. Marijuana first. Aerosols and glue were amazing. When I tried heroin I kept smoking until I puked, then I went right on smoking. Oh my God, the sheer relief and joy I felt. I developed a hacking cough that wouldn't go away. People told me to go see a doctor; they were fed up of hearing me. Made people sick, it did. But there was no way I was going to see a doctor. Then I took speed. Injecting. Then crack. But heroin was the best for the anger. I was terrified of anger, of being like my dad.

I started squatting once I left the children's home permanently. There was a house we broke into. A nice house in Camden in north London. It was empty but it seemed as though someone was trying to sell it because the estate agents came around the next day. We tried to ignore them, told them to get a court order, then we'd go, but they kept saying they wanted to come to some arrangement, so we talked.

The guy said: 'You leave in a week's time and we'll pay you a thousand pounds.'

I didn't believe him.

'We could take you to court but that would take time and almost as much money. We have a buyer lined up and don't want to tell him he can't move into his new home because it's being squatted. This way we cut out the middle men, get the house, sell it and you get a nice cash sum.'

We said yes. We got our stuff together, found another squat, cleared the house and then came back to wait for the agent, only to find two rough-looking builders fixing a steel door to the front of the house. We asked them about the estate agent. They told us to eff-off, so we did. Ripped off. From that moment rage burned within. I didn't know how I was going to control it. I got as high as I could but the rage stayed, and grew. I hit myself. Punching my head until I couldn't think straight. Then my stomach until I couldn't breathe. Then I pounded my legs with my fists until I couldn't walk.

The next day I went back to the house. It was mid-afternoon and no one was about; the neighbours weren't in, everyone was at work. The house was a big semi and I walked around the back, where I jimmied a window with a crowbar and climbed in, nice and easy.

I started in the kitchen. I had brought a 7.5kg mallet, one of the ones with the metal head. I smashed some cupboards, then took aim at the sink, pulling it off the wall until the pipes burst, then I attacked the oven, then the walls, smashing through plaster and pulling everything down. My rage was total. I kept going. I went to the top of the house and swung down on the top step until it snapped. Then I levered it out with the crowbar. I did that from top to bottom, so the stairs were impossible to climb, stopping only to smash up two bathrooms and put a few holes in the walls of each bedroom.

I walked away and came back a few hours later. The whole street was cordoned off. I'd broken a gas pipe. I felt good.

A mate of mine sold grass. He kept a stash of cash behind a bookshelf. One day he told me someone took it.

'You know who done it?' I asked.

'Yeah, this junkie, lives down in Camden, Pratt Street.'

Late at night. The two of us were outside the door. It was in a council block, a nice one, about five floors high. I took out my knife.

My mate looked panicked. 'I don't want any trouble.'

'Do you want your money back or not?'

The door was glass in a plastic and metal frame. I took out my knife and started to scratch grooves into the glass, etching 'junkie' in rough letters. The hall light came on and someone started running down to the door. They threw it open. A lanky blond man was standing there.

'What's happening?' he said, looking scared. 'What the fuck's going on?'

I took a step towards him and he saw the knife in my hand and backed off. He knew what was coming. He had it coming. At the sight of his pathetic, cowardly face, The Rage came down and I stepped forward. My mate was trying to hold me back but I pushed him away as I grabbed the blonde guy's outstretched arm and stuck the knife in. He screamed, so I took the knife out and punched him in the face. He was on the floor, crying, whimpering, pleading and then begging for mercy, crawling back towards the lounge. He'd give us the cash, he didn't have it right now. I put away my knife and picked him up, dragging him to the sofa.

My mate said he didn't want any part of this, and left.

I took out my knife and stabbed the thieving junkie bastard in the leg. He screamed and I punched him in the face again. I saw the blood and the mess he was in and it felt good. I yelled at him for a while and hit him some more, then turned and walked out. I kicked out the pane of glass in his door and walked down the stairwell and into the street. No one stopped me, no one saw me. If you have the guts, you can get away with anything in this town, I thought.

I had a girlfriend for a while. I don't know what she saw in me. She had dark hair, was a couple of years younger and from Denmark. Etta was her name. She came on to me. We had sex. It wasn't much good. But she liked heroin, too, and we could talk shit together and that was good. I got a job working for Dave, a dealer who lived in Mornington Crescent. He bought large weights and needed some psychos to make sure everyone who owed paid up and that no one tried to rip him off. He lived in a council block in his own flat and was loaded. The money was good and, as long as I made sure I was able to stand up when he needed me, he was happy with my work.

I didn't really have friends but Dave the dealer was the closest I got. He was ten years older than me, from Newcastle, and loved motorbikes. He had a huge motorbike that he'd ride up and down Camden and it sounded like hell had come to town every time he pulled up anywhere. We'd drink, do drugs and fight together. People were scared and got out of our way and I liked that.

So I hit, stabbed, burned and battered many people and I got a reputation. The violence came easy. I understood it, and pain, if someone managed to fight back and hit me, did nothing to stop me. I liked physical pain. It blocked out all the shit. But eventually I didn't have to do much of the beating up. Everyone just paid, if they knew what was good for them.

Dave was doing a big deal in a car park off the Finchley Road. His usual supplier had just lost a big consignment and so we needed to hook up with some other people in another part of town. I had my knife and a metal pipe. My head was shaved, I was six feet tall, twenty-three years old and had fists like a large pair of iron balls. I wore steel toecaps and dressed all in black. Everything about me said, 'Don't fuck with this guy: fucking with this guy would be a serious mistake that you would regret for the rest of your life.'

They fucked with us. Two cars. Theirs and ours. And a van that we never thought of checking, parked a little ways off. Men came out of it. They wanted Dave's money. Fuck them. I hit the man nearest to me as hard as I could and he went down cold. My hand was broken. When you face overwhelming odds, the secret of victory is to take them out quick and with deadly force. I kicked the guy in the head. Definitely out for the count. The next guy was Turkish-looking and didn't give me a chance to pull out my knife, so I sidestepped him and kicked him in the knee with my steel toecap and when he went down I was able to grab my knife and I stabbed him in the shoulder, twisting the blade. Then they were on me. I went rolling, down with men on me.

No escape.

Arms being held. Legs being held.

At some point, I understand that there will be pain. I spit and swear and tell them to get on with it, the chickenshits. Explosions start to take place. My knees, my balls, my chest and everything goes very bright and I stop breathing. I clench my teeth and feel my jaw is broken. Pain shoots everywhere in my body, from my skull to my little toe. I can't see what they're doing any more, I can't open my eyes. The pain is so great that I am in the moment, and am not conscious of anything else. I cry with happiness. The pain does not ease. It eats me up. I pray to no one and no thing. I take it, I take it all, until every last cell in me is screaming but all I can do is endure. No one individual moment is unbearable. I live moment to moment. Then weights and pressures are lifted and I am pushed, rolled down an embankment and everything goes black.

Part Two

WHAT'S LOVE GOT TO DO WITH IT?

THE LOVE ADDICTION

The stories in this book are shocking and unpleasant, which sometimes makes understanding and sympathising with the people telling them difficult. It is hard to understand how people can make disastrous life choices, such as turning to drugs and alcohol or falling in love with people who cause incredible emotional and physical pain.

Before we conclude the stories from Part One, it is worth considering the process that lies behind addiction as well as misdirected and destructive behaviour.

Most people don't understand addiction, even the addicts themselves. Addicts do not choose to become addicts. Addiction is the result of many complex processes involving biological, chemical, neurological, psychological and – vitally – social and emotional factors (and this is supported by decades of scientific research). But the key thing to remember is that addiction is extremely complex – and we should not judge drug addicts (even though this is sometimes impossible).

Drug addiction involves:

1. Compulsion and preoccupation with the drug/s of choice.

2. A lack of behavioural control.

3. Persistence, even when serious physical, emotional and social harm might result.

4. An extreme craving for the drug when it is not immediately available, which grows in intensity.

5. Promises to quit but quick relapses.

These are the key factors in any addiction (besides drugs, people can also be addicted to eating or having sex). Some never recognise their problem, while others do and accept the fact that their addiction will kill them unless they do something about it.

The first thing to understand is that drugs don't cause addiction. Addiction resides in the person who takes drugs – otherwise doctors wouldn't be able to offer drugs such as antidepressants and certain painkillers to anyone. Some people do become addicted to certain drugs after taking them just a few times but they are in the minority. Exposure to a mind-altering chemical does not make a person an addict. The person is already at risk. And once this person takes a certain drug, their descent into addiction is incredibly hard to stop as their tolerance quickly increases, and thereby their dependence. Tolerance is when an addict needs to use greater amounts of a drug to achieve the same high (and therefore spend considerably more money, often requiring more and more anti-social behaviours such as theft and prostitution to support the habit). You know you're dependent on drugs when you can't get hold of them, perhaps don't have enough money and, due to chemical changes in the brain, you start to suffer from withdrawal. It is dependency that starts to destroy you. About 80 per cent of opiate users relapse when they try to stop using.

Lack of control (powerlessness), lack of emotional interaction (love) and stress are the key factors that create the neurobiology required to kick-start addiction in people.

Recent advances in the knowledge of human brain chemistry have revealed the link between love and addiction. We know that the number of dopamine receptors is reduced in the brains of long-term drug users. Brain receptor molecules sit on the surfaces of cells where they receive a variety of chemical messages which instruct the cells how to behave. This interaction is necessary for our brain cells (and therefore our brains) to work normally.

Cocaine, along with other similar stimulants, leads to huge and sudden increases in dopamine – a chemical that makes the brain feel really, really good. It's this that leads the coke user's brain to produce wondrous feelings of untold possibility accompanied by superhuman exhilaration.

A key thing to remember is that a person with fewer dopamine receptors will *really* feel the high – as their brain welcomes something it feels has been missing for all of its existence.

Dopamine is also important in getting us out of bed in the morning – to motivate us to go and do something we believe in. People with lower numbers of dopamine receptors have less 'get-up-and-go' and are especially prone to addiction, particularly as more coke use leads to the loss of dopamine receptors and therefore more coke is needed for the next hit to reach the same levels of good feelings. This is because the brain, knocked off kilter by the drugs, is trying to regain its balance, and does this by reducing dopamine activity. Reduced dopamine activity (i.e. tolerance) adds to the pain of withdrawal, which involves fatigue, depression, feelings of paranoia and alienation, and it is this that leads to dependence. This happens with all common drugs: heroin, morphine, amphetamine, crack, alcohol, caffeine and nicotine.

Dopamine is a neurotransmitter. It crosses the gaps between the brain's synapses (the branches of brain cells that transmit information, known as the synaptic gap), sending messages to other brain cells. Once it has delivered its message, each dopamine molecule is taken back up into the cell from which it came, ready to be used again to carry its next message. Drugs like cocaine block the re-uptake of dopamine back into the cells from which they were originally released. They hover in the synaptic gap and it is this that creates the sense of joy and exhilaration. Natural activities that lead to an increased number of dopamine molecules in the synaptic gap include sex and eating.

Having sex doubles the amount of dopamine molecules but this is nothing compared to drugs like cocaine, which increases dopamine activity in the synaptic gap by 1200 per cent. After each use, the number of dopamine receptors will be reduced, so each time the user takes a mind-altering substance the brain has to work harder to get to the same high. Most drugs like cocaine provide a short high, only sticking around the receptor sites for a few minutes; as the buzz fades, the urge to take more is redoubled.

This change in the brain's state leads to drastic changes in the user's emotions and their everyday existence. This makes it extremely hard for the user to recover. The brain has to want to heal, to go back to normal, before the person can attempt to give up their dependency on a drug. The worse the addiction, the harder it is for the person to reach a decision that would be beneficial for their long-term health.

Opioid brain receptors that receive endorphins (a chemical which soothes emotional and physical pain – the word is derived from morphine), also welcome the presence of opiates such as heroin. Endorphins influence our mood (emotions), physical activity and immune system, and help regulate internal organs, including our heart. They play a key role in creating the emotional bond between mother and baby. Remove their opioid receptors and babies fail to connect emotionally with their mothers (this phenomenon has been observed in a number of animal experiments). Babies kept apart from their mothers start to suffer from separation anxiety. They can be soothed by being given opiates (again, this has been borne out through the study of animals).

When you think of, or experience, something sad, endorphins decrease in activity. Think of something happy and their activity increases. Similarly, when people think of relief (for example, are in pain but expect their pain to be relieved through the use of ibuprofen), endorphin activity increases in the opioid receptors, and the pain eases (known as the placebo effect).

Nurturing mothers experience major endorphin highs when they interact lovingly with their babies. These highs are designed to reinforce positive behaviour – the more positive behaviour, the more highs. To stop mothers from growing tolerant to these highs, their bodies produce a hormone called oxytocin (sometimes known as 'the love hormone'), which increases the sensitivity of the brain's opioid systems to endorphins. This way the brain doesn't try to restore a balance by reducing endorphin production. This is a key part of the mother-baby relationship. Without the wonderful feelings that come from providing everything their babies need, mothers would struggle with the otherwise unrewarding and exhausting task of parenting. Thanks to oxytocin, mothers are safely addicted to their babies.

Addicts who use opiates like heroin are messing with the brain system in charge of the most powerful dynamic in human existence: the attachment instinct.

Or, to give it another word: love.

It is important to note that opiates do not do away with pain. As effective as they may be, all they do is reduce our conscious awareness of it. Pain messages arrive in one part of the brain (the thalamus) which signals the anterior cingulate cortex (ACC), where we consciously become aware of it. Opiates work on the ACC by reducing the emotional impact of pain, rather than the pain itself. They dull the message.

In the real world, a baby may wake because she is in pain from teething, so her ACC receives a bunch of urgent and repeated messages from her thalamus. The emotions associated with the suffering of pain lead the baby to cry and the mother comes running. The appearance and soothing behaviour of the mother will lead the baby's brain to release endorphins, easing her emotional pain, just like an opiate would.

If the mother doesn't come, then the baby's brain won't release endorphins and she will try to find another way of coping – which will be ineffective, as only the release of endorphins will help. Some babies try to soothe themselves, others may suck their thumbs or rock back and forth. Children whose mothers rarely or never come running at these moments have a far higher chance of developing an opiate addiction as they approach adulthood and the opportunities for opiate use increase (at parties and nightclubs, or through their peers).

The number of opiate receptors, along with endorphin production, will decrease through underuse throughout infancy and childhood. The less endorphin activity, the greater the desire for narcotics such as heroin and cocaine – and alcohol. In essence, the more impoverished the brain's emotional centres, the greater the desire for chemical relief.

Because the life-foundational opioid love/pleasure/pain relief apparatus provides the entry point for narcotic substances into our brains, addicts most often express their first experience in terms of emotion. The drug 'hugs', 'comforts' and 'caresses' them; it 'lifts them up in its arms', it even 'loves' them.

Just to demonstrate how powerful the centres at which narcotics make their way into the brain are, consider the ventral tegmental area (VTA), which sits in the midbrain. When activated, it creates feelings of elation or desire. The VTA also triggers the release of dopamine in the nucleus accumbens (NA) at the front of the brain. These two brain components make up a system known as the incentive-motivation apparatus. It responds to reinforcement. All it takes for the NA to start firing off dopamine is a cue, something associated with a pleasurable experience one has had in the past. For drug users, those cues are people (fellow drug users), paraphernalia (the sight of a fresh needle or a crack pipe) and places (the dealer's house, street corner or pub). These triggers are so powerful that they often cause addicts who are trying to quit to relapse. Addicts often say how much they miss the process of getting high, from scoring the drugs to preparing the hit and, as hard as it is to believe, find these processes almost as hard to give up as the drugs themselves.

The processes described so far are all key parts of our limbic system, the emotional centre of our brain. They process emotions like anger, fear, happiness and love. Emotions are supposed to be able to help our survival. They tell us when to flee or fight and when to love or help a loved one. We are drawn to positives (love, food and water) and repelled by negatives (physical attack and poisons). For most people it runs perfectly, allowing beneficial social interaction, helping us to fall in love and protecting us from those who would do us harm. If the limbic system is damaged in some way then our emotions will do us more harm than good. Addiction is one of the most common and disastrous results of a damaged limbic system.

The prefrontal cortex (PFC), is one of the higher brain centres that deals with all of the intelligence processed by the rest of the brain and makes the decisions as to what we should do next. One of the key parts of this decision-making process is to reject all the bad decisions, i.e. inhibit inappropriate responses. The failure to recognise one bad choice can prove disastrous. People with damaged PFCs are unable to control their impulses and will act childishly and bizarrely.

Scientific studies have tied addiction to the orbitofrontal cortex (OFC), near the eye socket, which is closely and powerfully connected to the limbic system. The OFC decides moment-to-moment how we should respond, based on the emotional intelligence sent from the limbic system, to people and situations. It tells us whether to respond with love and is constantly assessing our relationships with other people – whether we should show them love or anger, for example. The OFC helps us inhibit harmful impulses (verbal or physical violence) and helps us balance short-term needs against long-term consequences. Many neuro-imaging studies (which record blood flow, activation and energy consumption) have shown that the OFC fails to do its job in the brains of drug addicts. Drug addicts are well known to accept short-term gains (getting high) over the risk of long-term pain (illness, damage to relationships, prison, their own career and financial stability). Addicts who say they cannot stop taking a drug, even though it has been a long time since it held any pleasure for them, are subject to the commands of the OFC, based on experiences the user can no longer consciously remember. The OFC has by this time been conditioned to create an irresistible urge to use, thanks to the creation of extremely robust neural networks, and it releases dopamine, increasing the addict's desire to use, displacing thoughts of unpleasant consequences.

So, as the brain develops, it is influenced by circumstances and events over which the child has had no control. In the case of children starved of love, their emotional brain never matures, so as adults they still respond like children in certain situations – with aggression and shouting. The same goes for their impulse control – it never develops. Brains like these are overwhelmed by narcotics, which are as close to a thing called love these people have ever known, and, before they know it, they are overcome by addiction.

As far as mammals go, humans are born with the most poorly developed brain, with only 10 per cent of the grey matter wired and ready to go – 75 per cent of human brain growth takes place after birth. From the moment the baby exits the womb, the brain starts to develop at an almost unbelievably rapid rate. Millions of synapses are created *every second*. By the time the baby is three years old, 90 per cent of its neurons are wired and ready for a lifetime of use.

Our experiences during this period are therefore crucial. The stimuli we receive determine *how* we're wired. The brain adapts to the environment it finds itself in. Those connections used most often grow strong while those that are ignored wither and die. What happens between the ages of zero and three years is the most important biological factor in terms of whether a child will grow up predisposed to addiction of any kind.

Nutrition, security and emotional nurturing are the key environmental factors that decide how well a baby's brain will develop. The baby's immature brain looks to the parents' behaviours to establish its own thought processes. It looks for any clue to learn about the outside world. These clues come from the way they're held, the way they're spoken to, the facial expressions of the people closest to them and, amazingly, even the size of the parents' pupils (the more dilated, the happier the person is and the better this is for the baby's development). Stressed parents raise stressed children, no matter how much they love them and how hard they try to do the right things.

Almost all addicts had tough starts to life and were predisposed to addiction because their parents, by abusing them sexually, physically or emotionally (perhaps just starving them of love), hardwired all the major brain systems necessary for addiction.

Imagine a child that no one ever smiled at, that never heard love in their parents' voices, was never cuddled or played with. Imagine the kind of adult that child would grow into. They would grow up at an extremely high risk of becoming dependent on drugs to make up for what their own brain is lacking.

Countless studies have revealed that most drug addicts have suffered from childhood traumas, such as sexual, physical and emotional abuse, domestic violence, the death of a parent, divorce, or drug/alcohol abuse. For each one of these experiences a person goes through, the chances of their becoming an addictive drug user are increased two to four times. For addictive alcohol use the rate is two to three times.

Physical and sexual abuse are perhaps the strongest predictors of addiction. Some people who have suffered childhood abuse and who are predisposed to addiction never find out. But for those who do finally try heroin or cocaine or alcohol, they are hit with overwhelming sensations of euphoria, comfort and security. Their experience is far more intense than for a 'normal' person. As well as the euphoria, they experience sudden and sheer relief from the anxiety and stress that has accompanied them throughout their life.

Addicts take drugs for respite from the emotional pain caused by the agonies they suffered in their pasts. But, on top of that, their past experiences have corrupted the development of their emotional brain.

As well as a permanent decrease in oxytocin production, lack of maternal contact leads to a permanent decrease in the mood chemical serotonin (stimulated by antidepressants). Decreases in serotonin lead to aggressive behaviour in adolescence and excessive consumption of alcohol, compared to their peers, while decreased oxytocin reduces a person's ability to establish loving attachments and long-term relationships – such people are more vulnerable to the overuse of drugs and alcohol as 'social lubricants'. The lack of supportive relationships only adds to the stress of the addict's life which, lacking clarity and control, is filled with uncertainty and this, in turn, enhances feelings of isolation and is likely to lead the addict to use the childlike behaviours of aggression and conflict during social interaction.

The damage that the lack of love can do to a child is far greater than most people imagine.

HOPE

I'm in a strange house. The bed is soft. My baby is beside me. It is safe. It has all the good smells of family – soap, clean washing, nice food, perfumes and deodorants – each one a luxury. The fear and pain are present but weakened for now.

I called the only number I had – Rebecca, the director of the fostering agency who'd once told me, 'If there's anything you need . . .' I don't think I needed anything so much as the help Rebecca gave me. As soon as I said, 'I can't cope in this place and I don't know what to do,' Rebecca drove up to see me that night and took me back to her house. I stayed with her, off and on, for a couple of months.

Rebecca managed to get Lauren and me into a house they used as a semi-independent home, even though it wasn't meant for a mother and baby, and persuaded me to see a good doctor, and we talked for a while.

'So you don't leave the house,' she said. 'You're crying all the time. You're in a permanent state of anxiety with regard to Lauren and are most worried about cot death.'

'Yeah, pretty much.'

That wasn't everything. Some of the social workers who'd been with me when I was still at the children's home had made a point of warning me against pregnancy. They made it clear that if I had a baby my life was over; that I wouldn't be able to go out and that my baby would be crying all the time and I'd have to spend every waking moment watching over her. I believed them and obsessed over Lauren; I was so scared something would happen that was out of my control. And top of the list was my irrational worry about cot death, which was far greater than I admitted to the doctor. I read everything I could get my hands on about this subject and would have probably given a world expert a run for their money in terms of my knowledge. I never let Lauren sleep in a cot. She was in bed with me, or right beside me in her carrier, so I could quickly check on her at any moment. I was convinced she was going to be taken from me – either through death or by social services.

'I think you have post-natal depression and need a little help,' the doctor told me. 'These pills will do it. Take one, three times a day.'

Chesterfields Children's Home: Report by the Educational Psychologist
10 May 1988.
Hope Daniels.
Age thirteen years and nine months.
She dismissed having any concern that she might develop an alcohol problem. (There is however the risk of identifying with her parents, especially when there is a distressing break in her

relationships in her substitutive home but I did not mention
this to Hope.)

I wouldn't admit it to anyone but I knew that I was at risk
of alcoholism from when I was a teenager. I could never
just have one drink, something inside me compelled me to
get blotto and then stay that way for as long as humanly
possible.

Alcohol was always an integral part of my parents' life
and it was the 'third person' in my relationship with
them. To feel its strong grip, coming in a rush of excitement that started in my heart and head, scared and
thrilled me. I didn't want to become my mother but, for
me, a drink was never just 'a drink'. Something in me
actually needed it, depended upon it and counted on it to
feed this desire.

I thought I could control it. And, after Lauren was born,
I knew I had to. Especially as I then fell pregnant with a
baby boy. Despite this, I was still alone. It was just me and
two babies. And, again, I stayed away from doctors and
the hospital until my eighth month. And, even though I
knew a lot more about having babies, the post-natal
depression hit me even harder. But this time I had a
wonderful midwife, a Jamaican lady called Beatrice with a
friendly motherly way. The kind of woman you just want
to hug, everyone's favourite aunt.

She knew enough to suspect that I might have some
issues after Joshua was born. I was scared of leaving the
hospital. I complained to Beatrice that my boobs were
really sore after breastfeeding and she said: 'You know a
trick for that?'

'No, what's that?'

'Geranium leaves.'

'You're crazy.'

'No, I'm serious. Put those on your breasts and it helps soothe them, really now.'

I don't know what it was, perhaps it was just Beatrice's straightforward kindness that tipped me over the edge, but something inside me broke and I burst into uncontrollable sobs.

'What is it, sweetheart?' Beatrice asked.

When I finally caught my breath, I said, 'You have to take my babies, I can't do it.'

'But why on earth not?'

'I will infect them, with my life and my mind. I will infect them. They can't be with their mum.'

Beatrice sat with me for hours as I sobbed and talked, telling her about my life, and she tried to talk me around but I just couldn't get my head to a point where I could imagine being a mum to these two beautiful little children.

Beatrice told me I would be fine and said she wasn't going to tell anyone if I didn't want her to but, as I left the hospital, I started haemorrhaging – which to me was another sign that I didn't deserve to have children – and I had to be brought back inside.

As I lay in recovery, Beatrice found me. 'You're going to go home and we've arranged for some health visitors to come around, just to make sure you're OK .'

Right then I felt as though I was incapable of even changing a nappy.

* * *

I waited patiently in my local social services' reception, with Lauren and Joshua sitting quietly in their pushchairs. A man in a suit, who looked like a police officer, was sitting, slouched in one of the chairs. He smiled and nodded hello.

I can't drink – but I have to.

I'd fought to control it and had managed. On my two allocated drinking days, Wednesday and Friday, once the kids were in bed by 7pm, I would drink from then until midnight, only drinking a carefully rationed supply I'd bought earlier that day – usually four bottles of beer. I knew that if I didn't drink from midnight until six in the morning, I'd be clear of alcohol and the day could begin as normal for the kids.

But the psychological price of this extraordinary routine of mine was too high, too impossible to live with. And the pain in the mornings, the emotional pain, as well as the hangover, was always stronger as my brain begged for a refill of the chemicals that numbed my feelings of emptiness, confusion and emotional despair. This methodical and controlled approach to drinking was exhausting.

I can't do this and be a mum to my children.

I had hung on for so long because I loved my children so much. When I was with them I was able to transform into supermum.

And then I realised that me loving these children was going to do them more harm than good.

My parents had loved us kids, despite their irrational and irresponsible behaviour that masked almost every last piece of affection. They had always wanted to see me, even when I didn't want to see them any more. Suppose I ended up like that? I didn't have the strength to keep up this way of life. I had no one to help, to relieve me and provide respite.

'Please take my babies.'

'Excuse me?'

'I can't do this any more. You have to take my babies. I can't cope.'

The receptionist had found me a social worker and we were sitting down with a cup of tea in a side room on the ground floor of the building. The sound of traffic came through an open window.

The social worker, a woman in her early thirties, looked at Lauren and Joshua. Lauren was playing as Joshua looked on.

'Looks like you're doing just fine to me. They're lovely. Tell me, why do you want to give them up?'

'I don't want to. I don't. I just can't. It's too difficult.'

I didn't tell them about my drinking. I didn't see that as the problem, I just talked about the feelings that were driving me to drink.

'Hope, we're not going to take your children from you but we can give you some help.'

Outside, in the real world, I wanted everyone to think I was all right and I kept people away, until the health visitor sent around by social services appeared. She was my saviour. Maria came around every single day for I can't remember how long. She was just amazing. It was like having a social worker without having the worry of a social worker. She gave me time when there were days I couldn't move, couldn't answer the door and Lauren would open it. She looked after the kids and helped around the house, checking I was up to date with all my bills and so on.

I never considered the idea that people didn't drink. Everyone liked to drink. I certainly did. And I continued to control it. Kids in bed. Sit down with my drinks ration and steadily work my way through them, longing for the feeling of numbness to come. But that feeling grew ever briefer. Come midnight, I staggered to bed, already sensing the hangover and the yawning emptiness that would come the next morning.

When the kids went to see their dad for the weekend, I drank for forty-eight hours straight and would wake up in the street, in the police station or in hospital. I was never violent when drunk (as least from what everyone told me). I was a risk to myself – as a young woman passing out in the roadside, falling and banging her head – and a temptation to abusers.

Come Monday I'd be back to 'normal' again.

It got worse the better my life got. I climbed out of my post-natal depression and got my life back on the rails and moved into a new house that I loved to bits and I kept it spotless, scrubbed within an inch of its life. Then, after starting out as a voluntary worker for a charity, I was offered a paid job for the Citizens Advice Bureau.

I helped the lost and lonely, addicts and homeless, advising and helping them as best as I could, and I loved it. I identified. Suddenly, life was going well – under control. I had a job that paid the rent and the bills and I looked after my children, who were loving school.

Then, in a pub one day, I met Danny. It was a

struck-by-lightning moment as I knew the second I saw him that I was going to marry him. I asked him out and he agreed. I was in love from that first moment. He was wonderful to me and loved the kids, who fell for him straight away. I hadn't been looking for anyone but something in Danny filled me with a desire to share my life with him. To give myself over completely – as I never do things by halves. We'd been together for a week when, one night, on my way home after seeing Danny, I took a minicab. I knew the driver quite well and asked him if he knew Danny. He did.

'I'm going to marry him!'

He looked at me like I was mad.

A couple of years later, Danny and I were walking through town when we bumped into the same taxi driver. We stopped to chat and he said: 'I met this girl a few months back and she said she was going to marry you!'

'That's right,' Danny said. 'We're getting married tomorrow!'

At the time, I thought I was the dog's wotsits. Life had its ups and downs but they were, as I saw it, mainly ups.

I continued to drink in my controlled fashion and managed to keep my excesses from Danny as he worked nights. The occasions when I appeared to be seriously the worse for wear, seemed to Danny to be widely spaced.

It is the nature of the addict to be deceitful. I knew this from my work but I could not see it in myself. It was just what I did to manage my drinking.

And then I got my files from social services.

The power that even the shortest phrase had on me was devastating. I broke down, not realising how hard these words would hit me – they were a sucker punch that left me reaching for bottle after bottle of wine in defence. Kill the pain. Kill the pain.

Deal with it. Alcohol.

I had been drinking too much for eight years. When Danny went to work and the kids were in bed, I started drinking. I was at the point where the shakes started to come on at 4pm, while I was still at work. I blamed everything else but my drinking. I found every excuse, from fatigue, too much coffee, needing a cigarette, being stressed, working too hard.

One night I ended up at a party in a horrible house, an old door on packing crates for a table, rotting carpets, loud, aggressive music, bad people. But there was alcohol. As much as I wanted to drink. So I kept going, kept the off-switch in my brain pressed firmly down, for as long as I could find a drink.

The police found me on the street, insensible. They put me in a cell and called Danny, who came from work to get me. Danny's step-dad had died from alcohol abuse and, although I'd been crafty hiding it from him, there came a point when it was obvious I had a problem. But if I didn't want to change, there was very little he could do about it except do everything he needed to so that the kids wouldn't notice – so that they wouldn't have bad memories of their mum the alcoholic.

A few times I would end up in dangerous situations. Most of the time I couldn't remember what had happened until the next day when Danny was telling me off, furious that I'd put myself in danger yet again, yelling at me, my head thumping, having landed on it again the previous night after toppling over, insensible, on a street somewhere in town.

Danny talked to me about going in for treatment and I went to the doctor, admitting finally that I was drinking too much. She suggested trying Alcoholics Anonymous. This, for me, didn't work. All the women there reminded me of my mum and so I hated going. I could only identify in the worst way – it reminded me of Mum and made me want to drink.

'You have to find something that works, Hope,' Danny told me.

I knew what that was but I didn't want to have to accept it. There was a local alcohol service that would take me. The only problem was that it was the one that I'd spent the last few years referring my clients to.

I made an appointment and I didn't turn up.

So I made another one.

And another.

And another.

And then I went on the binge to end all binges.

I wake up and the room spins. I'm lying in a strange bed and I can't move. I'm thirsty. God, I'm thirsty. Feels like I haven't drunk for days. The dizziness subsides and I start to shake uncontrollably. What's happening to me?

Someone comes in. A woman. I can't keep my eyes open long enough to discover anything else about her. My head hurts.

'Hope? You're awake. How're you feeling?'

Like shit. Like death.

I am thirty-four, the mother of two beautiful children, and I am in detox.

I shake, cry, sweat and shiver.

It is the summer of 2008.

I hallucinate. My brain is on fire with the contents of my social work files and won't let me rest. Suddenly, I am fourteen years old, demanding to see my social worker from Chesterfields Children's Home. They will explain to me what's going on.

The woman touches my head. I flinch, shivering, stuttering. I try to say something else but it's lost in the shakes. I'm scared. I try to tell her, I'm sick, something's really wrong.

'Hope, do you know where you are?'

Of course. I'm fourteen years old and I've been put in the secure unit. I see the files, the old typewritten pages:

Calakow House Secure Unit: Hope Daniels (14 years old) was admitted on 25.3.88 on a secure order, following repeated absconding from Chesterfields Children's Home . . .

'The secure unit—'

I shouldn't be here. I should be in Chesterfields, where I made them promise to find me a family.

Request for long term foster home:
She is a well-built girl with blue eyes, pale complexion, short, light-brown hair. She looks mature, well beyond her years. She has a most attractive lively appearance. She presents in a polite, pleasant and mature way but really lacks confidence and is emotionally quite fragile. She is vivacious, sharp and humorous in manner. Warm and affectionate.

Hope desperately wants to be part of a normal family and experience warmth and affection and being special to

*someone. However, she will pose problems and ideally should
be placed with really experienced foster parents.*

The voice comes as if from a far-off world: 'You're dehy-
drated, Hope. Can you try to drink a little water? Just a
few sips?'

A cup is pressed to my lips. My shakes turn to convulsions. I try to open my eyes to see the cup so I can push it
away with my hands but my hands won't do what they're
told. The convulsions make me want to vomit and I sit up,
and this time when my eyes open I see Mum in front of me
with a drink in her hand, fag in her mouth, looking at me,
angry. What have I done?

*Mr and Mrs Daniels . . . seemed quite out of touch with their
children's needs and did not seem to think that, as parents,
they might alter their drinking behaviour . . .*

> *They have been chronically impoverished . . .*
> *helpless . . .*
> *long cycle of prison sentences . . .*
> *Both have experienced very poor parenting and it seems
> they have never learnt to be good parents themselves . . .*

Mum speaks, she seems to be pushing the cup at me. 'Why
did you leave, Hope? Why did you leave?' My eyes hurt,
my head hurts, my stomach hurts and vaults, and I retch. I
try to ask how I got here but it comes out as a moan. What's
wrong with me?

I open my eyes, figures swim in and out of view. Dad
is here, too. What are you doing here, Dad? I told you not
to come.

Neither parent has seen Hope for about six months. Hope is reluctant to have contact with them because of their frequently drunken and abusive behaviour . . .

Mr and Mrs Daniels express ambivalence towards Hope – they express a desire to see her but are very angry that she has not wished to see them. Mr Daniels, in particular, has absolutely no insight into Hope's needs and the impact of their behaviour and attitudes on her.

Dad is holding my hand. He is saying something, trying to speak, but my stomach twists and turns and I fold in two.

Her father Mr T. Daniels is a 66-year-old man who was himself in care between the ages of three and 16 years. It appears he had an unhappy childhood and was placed in an approved school from the age of 10 . . .

He has no experience of being parented. He was returned to his father and stepmother at the age of 16 where he discovered he had three younger brothers, close to his own age, which further increased his sense of being abandoned and neglected . . .

He admits to multiple prison admissions following charges for shoplifting and living off immoral earnings offences . . .

He says that his level of alcohol intake has increased since his children were taken away and he expresses a sense of boredom with life. He has not sought help with his alcohol problems.

Mum is saying something like: 'You're just like me, you're just like me,' over and over again.

'I'm not, I'm not like you, Mum. I'm not, I'm not, I'm not.'

'But you're in the secure unit, Hope,' she answers. 'Same one they put me in.'

I scream with pain.

Mrs Daniels is 49 years old and the youngest of four children . . .

She is separated from her nearest sister by 13 years. She was close to this sister who died of a brain tumour when Mrs Daniels was 19.

Mrs Daniels's father . . . had a history of alcohol abuse and was absent throughout most of her childhood.

Mrs Daniels herself ran away from school and from several children's homes. She was placed in Calakow House Secure Unit for assessment as a teenager . . .

Her first child was born when she was twenty-one and was subsequently adopted . . .

She met Mr Daniels, some fifteen years her senior, when she was twenty-five years old . . .

There have been a variety of problems resulting in removal on some three occasions . . .

Mrs Daniels gave birth to Phillip alone in a furnished room . . .

Mrs Daniels, like her husband and father, has a long history of alcohol abuse. She admits to long prison sentences for shoplifting and being drunk and disorderly. I understand that she previously worked as a prostitute. It seems, from Hope's account, that Hope has been exposed to her mother's sexual activities . . .

Hope describes clients being brought back to the family home where space was very limited when her mother 'thought she was asleep'.

I want to get up but my legs feel like lead. My joints ache. And the taste of wine is on my tongue. I'm cold, freezing. I try to say, 'Can I have a hot water bottle, please?' and eventually manage, 'Hot water bottle.'

My dad leans in, touching my forehead. 'But you're so hot, Hope. You've got a fever.'

Since when do you care? I think, squinting at the old man. Sweat stings my eyes. I look past him. Something about this room. Shadows dart back and forth across the pulsing walls. I don't deserve to be here. I close my eyes.

All three children were admitted into care in 1983 . . .

Wards of court . . .

Resident at Chesterfields Children's Home for the last four years . . .

Hope had become attached to care staff and settled well . . .

Changes of staff . . . began using alcohol and cigarettes . . . some re-enactment of her mother's history . . . absconding at night and putting herself at risk . . . no account of where she spends these nights . . .

Since admission to Calakow, she has experienced poor peer relations and has retreated . . .

Bright flashes of light. Red, gold, blue. My eyes are closed but the lights are as bright and more intense than fireworks. My heart thuds like a bass drum, echoing. My skin itches but when I try to scratch, hands pull my arms away.

Ashamed of her parents . . .

Sorry for them rather than angry . . .

Particularly about her mother's prostitution and her disgust at the idea of 'selling her body' . . .

Does not miss her parents . . .

Would prefer not to see them . . .

She denied any interest in alcohol and is not afraid of developing a drink problem . . .

She evidences no signs of disturbed sexual behaviour (apart from speaking in a crude manner) . . .

She has consistently expressed the desire to be fostered and has some understanding of the possible difficulties . . .

She might continue to abscond . . .

She is also at grave risk of developing an alcohol dependency disorder . . .

The tendency to re-enact her mother's history, which she is at risk of repeating.

'Don't struggle, Hope, just relax, relax, relax.'

The flashing lights slow down and everything is silent, I open my eyes but it's like they're weighed down with bags of sand. I try to focus. Figures move. There's a strip light that flashes at me in slow motion. I feel my jaw go slack and my lids slam shut with a thud . . .

August 1987 – Hope was charged with shoplifting . . .

September 1987 – A pattern of absconding started, which has since accelerated . . .

October 1988 – The police were called to the home during the night because Hope and another girl were quite uncontrollable and were also damaging the property . . . Both girls were arrested . . .

A man's voice: 'Hope? Are you OK ?'

The sheets hurt. My skin is raw.

Another voice: 'Hope, Do you know where you are?'

'Secure unit.'

'What year is it?' the stranger's voice asks. 'How old are you?'

1982. Eight.

> *Mrs Daniels, Hope's mother, was sent to an approved school when she was 14 years old because of truanting. She often absconded and when she was 16 years old she spent a year in a closed ward in a psychiatric hospital, she has no idea why . . .*

> *An older man got her pregnant . . .*

> *The child was put up for adoption shortly after birth . . .*

> *There were family rows about her father's heavy drinking . . .*

> *Mrs Daniels earned some money by soliciting and Mr Daniels served two prison sentences for living off immoral earnings . . .*

> *Evicted from their flat due to soliciting . . .*

> *Both Mr and Mrs Daniels gradually increased their alcohol intake . . .*

> *They had a daughter when their oldest son was two years old but, due to their situation, they felt it would be best if she was adopted . . .*

> *Difficulties with neighbours . . .*

> *Current accommodation . . . very poor state of repair . . .*

> *Mrs Daniels has appeared on several drunk charges this year . . .*

> *Theft of a bottle of whiskey . . .*

> *Feels helpless when considering whether she can change her habit or behaviour . . .*

Both Mr and Mrs Daniels drink regularly to a state of intoxication. They assure me that this only occurs on Monday, Tuesday and Wednesday and that they can still care for their children . . .

Mrs Daniels and the family are clearly in need of help and their future is bleak if the present situation continues . . .

It seems likely that they are both brain damaged by drink . . .

Unwilling and unable to recognise that their drinking is the cause of their troubles.

'Her blood pressure is high, but she's improving.'

'Can I talk to her? Can she hear me?'

'Yes, but I'm not sure she'll understand everything.'

'Hope, Hope, can you hear me? You're going to get better. You're going to come home soon.'

All three children very much want to be fostered. They do not want to spend the rest of their childhood in a children's home.

When I interviewed Hope she was most anxious that her future placements would not be open-ended and that the Local Authority would make a serious attempt to find foster parents for her.

What progress has been made?

The initial referral to fostering and adoption was on 17.10.1985.

Nothing was achieved . . .

No prospect in the foreseeable future . . .

Attempts to foster would have to be dropped . . .

Indications that Hope, in particular, was not happy with this . . .

Her parents, particularly Mrs Daniels, would undoubtedly do their best to destabilise any placement and their behaviour alone would put pressure on a foster placement . . .

This was always sufficient reason for not attempting it . . .

Harold and Hope are now 13 and 14 respectively so time is getting short . . .

Adolescent problems are present . . . truanting . . . thieving . . .

They have fairly unrealistic expectations of fostering, i.e. Kellogg's Cornflake packet picture of family life and high materialistic expectations . . .

Decision must be made one way or another – uncertainty is very unsettling for the children.

I open my eyes. They are dry, my lips are cracked and they sting when someone presses a cup to them.

'Take these.'

Two pills are pushed into my mouth.

'These are going to stabilise your heart, get your blood pressure down and hopefully reduce your urge to vomit. You have to take them every few hours, there's some unpleasant side effects, but I'll reduce the strength over time. I need to take some blood and run a couple of tests, make sure all your insides are OK. You'll be up and about in no time. Promise.'

I open my eyes and twist in the bed. I put my hands to my head and then lift them off. I look at my hand. The tattoo is there but it's faded, it's just a blue smudge, already.

Wait . . . ?

I look across the room and see Dan. He tells me he loves me. That I've been here for four days and nights.

My files. I read my social service files. I thought I was ready. Then three bottles of wine and then after that . . . I don't know.

My mum was in the secure unit. I was in the secure unit. My mum and dad were alcoholics.

I am an alcoholic.

My mum lost all her children.

For a while it felt as though my head had left my body and was floating away; it felt dreamy, pleasant. For those who were near me at the time, I was shaking and retching, barely conscious and barely breathing.

The first night was just about keeping me alive and on the second night, the shaking frenzy set in. It got so bad that I needed to be knocked out and, as I drifted between various states of non-conscious awareness, the experience triggered more memories of being in care.

Danny and the nurses kept trying to explain where I really was but I could only see Mum and Dad and my room in the secure care home – and my belief only grew stronger as my system screamed for the alcohol that had kept so many of those feelings in check; aided by the medications they fed me to help my body cope.

And a few days later, after being weaned off the medication and, as I was regaining consciousness, I committed to a six-month alcohol programme at the Kenward Trust, where I'd missed countless appointments.

At first, I still didn't believe them when they told me how bad I was. I thought I needed help so that I could be all right with my drinking and not get out of control again.

They soon set me straight. It was time to quit.

I was lucky, they said. I could have killed myself through alcohol poisoning. If I continued to drink like I had done, I would die.

Presented with no choice, i.e. this or death, I agreed to end it forever.

As I regained my senses, I felt the old, unstoppable fear that social services were going to show up, just as they had done when I was a little girl, except that this time they were going to take the kids away from me and Danny would go with them.

The fear had to stop. I knew it. But I didn't know how. I had to deal with my past, with being in care and the loss that went with it – the loss of childhood and my family. Otherwise I would be sober and have to live with all these emotions and fears. There was nothing else to do. I had to let myself go, open up and talk; talk about things I'd never said to anyone before.

Emotional maturity stops when the trauma starts. My trauma had started early. For the first six months I regressed to the state of an enraged teenager. I threw chairs, argued, swore and refused every suggestion. I had never had the chance to grow into an adult. I didn't know how. There were more things about life that scared me than I even knew about. From that fear came rage.

It took months. Months of reacting to insights as a teenager, rather than as a grown-up wife and mother of two children.

I thought that if my children found out about my life in care and my drinking, that they would detest me. That I was a failure as a human being. I also thought it was my fault that our family had ended up in care. I had gone with my brothers to the police station when our family life broke down.

I argued against all the good things they pointed out about me. I just couldn't hear them. And then I'd leave and be scared that the treatment wasn't working.

Outside of the treatment centre, I was unable to leave the house. My own splendid isolation.

'Come on, Hope,' Dan said. 'Why don't we go out? Just for a drive. You won't even have to step out of the car.'

'I can't. What if I lose it and jump out and start screaming in the street? Suppose I have a drink?'

'I'll make sure that won't happen.'

I shook my head and stayed sitting on the sofa, hugging my knees, waiting for the fear to end. What is happening to me? Why can't I control anything?

The only time I felt safe outside of home was at the treatment centre. I could lose control there. Say anything. Do anything (just about).

And then I arrived at my therapy session one day and they'd brought out some puppet figures.

'Oh, for God's sake,' I said. 'Dolls? Seriously?'

I went along with it and, suddenly, I could see myself as a kid, with my brothers, and something caught at the back of my throat. I felt so sorry for us. It was so sad. Then there was this pain in my throat and I gasped. What was going on? I felt tears in my eyes. But I never cried, never. And I collapsed into sobs; it was unstoppable, nearly hysterical. I didn't know how to stop.

That was the first day I felt a total release. I let go of my past and understood that what had happened was all in my past. Something, as a result of all those months in therapy and staying clear of alcohol, had caused a huge shift in me.

Before, I'd believed that to forgive myself and my mum and dad was just a way of letting us all off the hook; that I was condoning everyone's behaviour. Instead of forgiveness, I carried an iron ball of resentment – and it had stayed with me for all of my adult life. My way of coping and getting through life was to ignore what had happened. The anger in me came out as energy to get on with my life, while the drink shut up the voices inside that wanted to be heard – the voice that belonged to young Hope, that little girl who walked into a police station almost twenty-five years ago. When I stopped drinking, I had to let her out.

And that was my breakthrough. Even today, people can't understand how and why I've forgiven my parents, but it's the only way to create peace of mind. That's what I have now. These days, when I have a flashback, I feel incredibly sad for us as kids, and sad for Mum and Dad.

The anger isn't there any more. I'm free.

JOHNNY/JEMMA

I begged for and got a job in a clothes shop but had nowhere to live until the clubs opened and I could go home with any random guy that would have me. One night a boy told me about a trust that fostered gay and lesbian people – the carers were all lesbian and gay themselves and, being sixteen years old, I still qualified. So I went to see them and, after about three weeks, I was fostered.

Matt was in his forties, tall, slightly overweight and had a salt-and-pepper beard. He lived alone in a small three-bedroom house in west London. He'd been involved in charity work for most of his life and seemed nice but I couldn't bring myself to trust him. I couldn't see anyone I lived with as not abusing me because that's all I'd known. Even if I'd been living with Mother Teresa I would have expected her to attack me at some point. Matt knew I was gay and although I was trying to act the tough guy and be all butch, I became obsessed with the expectation of abuse and it reached the point where I was analysing the slightest noise in the house at night, thinking he was coming to get me – any sound was a potential threat and I spent the whole time on alert.

I was sitting quietly in the bath, bubbles everywhere, and was lying back with my head on the rim, eyes closed, when I heard a noise. I opened my eyes and saw the door opening – I had forgotten to lock it! I screamed as loudly as I could as Matt came through. He retreated instantly at the noise. 'Oh, jeez, sorry, Johnny,' he said. 'I didn't know you were in there. The house was so quiet I thought you were out.'

Not long after this, we were in the middle of a brief summer heatwave and I walked into the kitchen when Matt was having his morning coffee and saw he had his top off. I started to shake and I could barely talk as I tried to fight the urge to run away. Instead, I walked out of the house calmly, telling myself that it was OK; Matt had shown me nothing but kindness from the first day. Nothing had happened but still the fear, the desperation, had a strong hold of me.

I loved fashion and went around London's fabulous charity shops picking up all sorts of clothes and I dressed in all sorts of styles, from cowboy chic to mod, and Matt would watch my fashion parades as I changed and showed him in front of the mirror what I was wearing. Matt redecorated the house and allowed me to do my own room – I painted the walls turquoise and the floorboards white and neon orange.

'Every day is an adventure with you,' Matt said, chuckling, when I showed him the finished room. Gradually Matt became part of my life; he took on the role of a dad unconditionally and when I hit the clubs and still wanted to party beyond dawn, Matt would pick me up at 3am and drive me to Trade, a club that opened at 5am on a Sunday, where the party continued. 'Have you been taking drugs?' he'd ask and, with saucer eyes on stalks, I always told him, No, of course not. Matt knew, but said nothing. He'd read the Sunday papers and have coffee and breakfast at a nearby cafe until I was ready to go home and sleep. Matt was there for me but he let me be at the same time. As the trust grew, I started to love him as a son loves his father. I was finally enjoying life – I worked in fashion and was making enough money to enjoy the party scene and, for the first time in my life, I had a secure home, somewhere I felt safe with a man who loved me for who I was and nothing more.

Maybe because of this security I started to really think about living as a girl again. I didn't think I could live that way in London, after the last time I'd been beaten up, so I looked for a place where people could really be themselves and no one would care.

The answer, it seemed, was New York.

Matt came to pick me up from the airport. My friend George was there but I was not.

'Johnny's staying in New York,' he told Matt. George was a platonic friend and we'd gone for a holiday but I'd been blown away by that crazy city from the moment we stepped out of the subway and into Manhattan. It was immediately obvious that, here, I could live as a girl and, after managing to get a job that paid cash-in-hand in a shoe shop, I found a small apartment in Queens and started to live as a transsexual. Once I had the job and an address, I managed to extend my visa for six months.

I called Matt 'Dad' now and when he came over to see me I told him. 'Dad, I want to live as a woman, and here is a place I can do it.' I went to my bedroom and got changed. After taking a deep breath, I opened the door and braced myself.

'You're beautiful,' Matt said. 'Like Audrey Hepburn.' It was true. I was petite and beautiful; you never would have thought I had lived most of my life as a man. We ate out that night in Chelsea as father and daughter. I called myself Jemma and, even as we listened to the three-piece jazz band, I told Matt just how much he meant to me and just how much he'd done for me – from being the first person to feed me decent food, to being the first person to let me be truly myself.

Matt told me my metamorphosis hadn't come as much of a shock and, now, seeing me as I was, he couldn't imagine me as anything other than a woman. I cried with happiness. But the freedom to live as a woman in New York came at a price. I wasn't able to make friends and New York was a lonely place for someone eking out a living on a low wage. But I didn't want to return home; to do so would have been a failure. I found it harder and harder to cope with the loneliness, though, and started to pluck my hair, an impulsive disorder called trichotillomania. The tension and relief of pulling then plucking was somehow satisfying to me, an instant pain-reward exchange; a quick gratification at any given moment.

I needed more money and so I tried sex working but it didn't happen. The men and women selling themselves on the street had incredible bodies and took confidence to a whole other level, while I looked like a crazy person – I'd grown and dyed my hair and fashioned it into dreadlocks, and I'd pierced everything I could. I walked into an alternative kind of club where I asked for a job as a dancer and, after the manager ran his eyes up and down me a few times, he asked me to 'Show what you got'. So I did and got the job. My freakish good looks worked in my favour this time. My dress became more outlandish, so much so that even in New York people started to pass comment on the subway. Eventually, I grew so lonely and I desperately missed Matt, thousands of miles away, the one person who cared for me. Suddenly, I felt like Matt was 'Home'. For the first time in my life I was able to call something home without it having horrible connotations. It had taken six months in New York for me to realise this. I got together enough money for a ticket back to London.

It wasn't the same. Something had happened to me since going away. In part, I felt like a failure for coming back and I fell into a depression. I took an overdose. The doctors wanted me to talk to a shrink.

'It might help,' Matt advised when I came home, bone thin, shaking, as if I were ready to crack and fall into a million tiny pieces at any second.

'Your female side is part of a personality disorder,' the shrink said. 'I'd like you to take some pills to help.'

These were male hormones, designed to bring out my male side. Even now, it seemed as though the medical profession were determined to force me to be a man and, from a lack of strength or lack of light in the other direction, I went with it. From that moment on, I took drugs every day I could and went out every single night. Sometimes I'd dress as a woman but I'd return home feeling ashamed and would dress up as a boy, go out all butch and pull a man. And all of the time, I kept my eyes out for Simon, searching for him in the clubs and bars of the West End.

I started to develop a personality disorder; I felt as though there were two of me. I'd ask myself who I was going to be that night and with these two characters pulling me one way, then the other, and with muscles growing and the hormones, I decided that it was time to leave this world in which I could not make myself fit. There was no forcing it and, as much as I loved Dad, I just didn't have the strength to live.

By now I had no hope of ever being a woman, my head was shaved and I had big muscles – I couldn't look more butch. I'd done everything I could to live as a man but my soul belonged to a woman who wouldn't leave me in peace, and so I decided to travel to Ibiza for one last blast and then, at the end of the holiday, my plan was to overdose myself to oblivion.

I liked the fact that no one knew me there and the idea of being away from the mess of my life appealed to me. On the first day, I saw a guy selling tickets for snorkelling trips and so I bought one on a whim. The boat trip was already beautiful before we got to the snorkel spot; everything you'd want from Ibiza – the sky was blue, the sun was high but the light wasn't harsh, just bright enough to make the sea, which was clear, glitter and shimmer, the sandy island was a jaggy rock behind us. Snorkels and flippers on, we dropped into the water. It was like swimming in Evian, it was that clear. Fish were everywhere, paying me no mind. Nothing I could say or do would bother them. What a way to be. After the session was over, I said I wanted to go on the next trip, and it was then I realised that I didn't want to die. I wanted to be me. I had been through so much, lived so much already. I could be me, I really could. I don't know if anyone else has ever been left feeling so rejuvenated by a boat ride and a bit of snorkelling; certainly when I saw the young man handing out leaflets for the trip again, my smile was so wide I'm sure he thought I'd fallen head over heels in love with him. From that day, I stopped using drugs.

Back in the UK, I leapt into another relationship, this time with a wonderful man. When I saw a TV documentary about a transgender person I made sure we watched it; I was ready to tell him afterwards that I was transgender and was going to become a woman but, before I could, he blurted out at the screen: 'That's ridiculous! You're a gay man, live like one.'

'Don't you think he has a right to be who he feels he is rather than what society dictates?'

'No way, it's just too fucking weird.'

'Suppose I wanted to do that?'

'You?' he laughed. 'You're way too masculine to pull that off.'

As much as I liked him, I couldn't stay with someone who felt like that, so I dumped him. I was walking the streets a short time later when I saw a transgender person selling the *Big Issue*. I bought one and, flicking through the magazine on the tube, I spotted an ad for drug worker training, supporting people who were trying to break their addictions and rebuild their lives. Three hundred people applied for twelve places. I was one of the twelve.

At the end of the first day's training, I told everyone: 'Today I came in as Johnny. Tomorrow when I come in, I'm going to be Jemma.' I could see from their expressions that I'd ruffled some feathers, but they were just going to have to deal with it.

To be honest, I looked like a man in a wig at the beginning but, ignoring curious looks, I plunged on into the training, which went really well. I soon found work once the course was completed, even going on to win awards. After all, I was once a user; I knew better than most what people were going through in their struggles with addiction and why they felt compelled to use something so harmful time and time again.

Gradually my muscle tone changed, I grew more slender, my hair grew long and people started to see me as a woman. I met a wonderful man who did nothing but support me when I decided to have the operation. By this time I was a force to be reckoned with. I wasn't about to take any nonsense from a doctor who hadn't the slightest clue what it was like to be in my position. The way I saw it, the NHS had got me into this mess and it was up to them to sort it out.

They tried but the operation was not a success. Because there wasn't much of a penis to work with, it made the surgeon's job difficult and, after I woke up, sore and thirsty as hell, I was welcomed back to the world with the news that I was going to have to use a catheter.

I went home and, behind my wonderful boyfriend's

back, I started to look for Simon. Even though it had been seventeen years, I remembered my promise. He was the first man to love me and I had loved him so much, I still thought about him every day.

And this time, I found him.

Simon was on Facebook. I immediately ended it with my boyfriend and messaged Simon, telling him I was now a woman and he could have me as his wife. I said he was my first love and I would always love him, and that I would live with him forever. He responded, asking to meet, and I travelled to see him on the train.

I almost didn't recognise him. When he smiled, half his teeth were missing. He was old, withered, hunched and balding. 'My God, he's had a hard life,' I thought. We walked to a hotel where Simon told me a sob story of drug addiction and alcoholism, how his family had suffered, driving him to drugs to escape.

I said he should move in with me and I would help him get better. After all, I was a drug worker, right? What better person could there be to look after Simon and make him better?

I still saw Dad regularly but I never told him about Simon. I knew he wouldn't approve and that he would try and make me see sense. I didn't want to see sense; I wanted to be with the man I loved more than I wanted to listen to the man who loved me like his own child.

From the start I was blind to Simon's crimes. He started sneaking out of the house to 'get me a Starbucks' when he was actually going to meet a heroin dealer.

It wasn't until I arrived home from work to find I'd been

burgled and Simon was nowhere to be seen that I realised. He turned up a few days later, the money he made by selling my possessions for peanuts had all been spent on drugs. I lost it when I saw him, and he sat quietly while I ranted and raved, until I ran out of steam. Then he stood up, walked slowly over to me and belted me as hard as he could in the stomach. Catching me totally by surprise, I fell, gasping for air and then, as I lay there helpless, Simon kicked me between the legs. He was a big guy with heavy boots and my wounds were still sore from the surgery. I couldn't get up for an hour.

Even though Simon was a total psychopath I still believed I could change him, and that he would get better with time. Of course it would be tough and harsh in the beginning, I reasoned, but the longer he stayed with me, the better his chances were.

Simon started to beat me regularly. My job was all about fixing people's lives and here I was making a total mess of mine. There were happier times – when he was high or had access to drugs – when he poured out his heart to me, praised me, told me how sorry he was, that the drugs had made him into this monster. And then, a few days later, he'd punch me in the face because I wouldn't give him money for drugs.

We lived this way for three years and nothing changed. We moved house and, out of shame and fear, I didn't see Dad for three years. I couldn't bring myself to go because I knew I was failing and falling apart, and because I knew Dad would want me to leave Simon.

We eventually met at a rooftop bar when my relationship with Simon was at its most abusive.

'It's not too late to stop this guy,' Dad told me after I described some of my life with Simon. 'I know you had to be with Simon, he was too important a person in your life not to, but now you must see, it's time to slay this monster that has been in your life for so long. For too long.'

There was nothing I could say. I felt so helpless. It was impossible to leave Simon; he would never let me go.

'I'll be there whatever you do,' Dad said, with tears in his eyes. 'Whatever you decide and whatever happens.' I think he felt that Simon was going to end up killing me. We hugged for a long time and when I finally said good-bye, I felt like I might never see him again.

It took me a year to persuade Simon to go to a drugs reha-bilitation centre close to where I worked. My colleagues knew I was transsexual and I'd not been able to hide the beatings from them. 'He's made all the promises I need to hear,' I told a work colleague after Simon went into rehab.

She just shook her head. 'Some people are bad through and through, and there's nothing you can do.'

A few days before Simon's six-month stay in rehab was up, I was due to have another round of surgery to try and fix the problems caused by the last attempt. I really wanted to talk to Simon before I went in but when I called the centre they told me that he'd refused family therapy; that he didn't want to talk to me.

I told them that Simon had called me up just a few days earlier, telling me how much he loved me and how happy we were going to be once he got out. 'I'm sorry, but he's been very clear.'

He was still messing with me, even while he was in

rehab. That should have told me something. But love is blind.

When Simon got out, a few days before my operation, it was as if nothing had changed. He took drugs and beat me up; a neighbour called the police when I screamed for help, and he started to strangle me before they arrived. When the police did finally turn up, Simon quickly calmed down and told them: 'She hasn't taken her meds.' The officers looked at me. I knew not to say anything because Simon would find a way to make me pay if I did. 'I'm taking care of her,' Simon said. 'She needs to give me one hundred pounds to get groceries and pay the bills.' The police sided with Simon and went away, but not before they let him take my key. Simon called me up later that night, high and laughing at me, from a friend's house.

Some months earlier, once I had received the date of the operation, I'd booked a holiday for Simon and me in Ibiza. It was supposed to be a reward for Simon going through rehab and a place for me to recover from the surgery – I wanted to return to the island where I'd been reborn.

Between work, Simon and all the associated emotions that came with the impending operation, I was exhausted by the time the holiday was due to start. Nevertheless, I still thought I'd put so much effort into this relationship, that even if I had the smallest chance I had to stick it out.

The night before I was due to have the surgery, Simon went out, coming back at six in the morning. I went downstairs to wait for the taxi to take me hospital, alone.

I had the operation and, although some things were fixed, I was still pretty weak by the time we left for Ibiza. I had all the medications I needed and was really looking forward to the sun. I planned to take trips around the island to various beaches and lie, reading and recuperating. Simon said he'd rather stay by the hotel pool. I knew he was going to look for drugs but I couldn't face an argument, so I left him to it.

On the second day I had just left the hotel when I realised I'd forgotten my purse, so I returned upstairs. The door to our room was still open. Simon was sitting on the sofa, where I'd left him, with his back to me, but now he was shaking and moaning. My laptop was next to him on the sofa and I saw he was masturbating to child porn.

I thought he was going to beat me to death when he turned and saw my horrified face. I was weak from the operation, my wounds were sore and weeping. The only thing I could think of to say was a lie: 'I've just had a call from the rehab centre. They're prepared to take you back. I'll get you a flight back to London. If you stay here, then I'm going to leave.'

To my amazement, he agreed. The only catch was there was no rehab and I had no money left for a flight. I called Dad.

'Don't worry,' he said. 'I'll send the money by Western Union now.' The money arrived, I asked the hotel to help me book a flight and, still to my amazement, Simon actually went. When I got back to the room, I realised I couldn't stay there for another moment. I didn't want to be in the same space that man had been. I asked the hotel to transfer me, which they did, and I started to pack but, as I did, I began to feel dizzy and blacked out.

I woke up on the bathroom floor with a huge bruise on my forehead. This moment was rock bottom for me – so I thought. By the time I was able to make it to bed, Simon had left a dozen messages on my phone. He'd landed in London and was threatening me with everything under the sun, from abuse to destroying my home, and accusing me of having affairs and deliberating infecting myself with HIV so I could pass it on to him.

Feeling too weak to stay in Ibiza on my own, I found a pay phone (my mobile was barred after Simon had racked up a load of charges calling a teenage boy he'd had an affair with while in rehab) and called Dad, who came to the rescue once again, sending me £500 so I could come home early. I spotted Simon sitting on my doorstep smoking a cigarette and told the taxi driver to keep driving.

I went to the only place I could – to see Dad.

Dad came with me to the police station and, after about an hour's wait, we were ushered into an interview room with two young male police officers.

'So you say this man, a drug addict, with whom you've been living for some years now, hit you when you were recovering from an operation, some weeks ago.'

'Yes.'

'And you caught him watching child pornography on your laptop, in another country, a few days ago.'

'Yes.'

The two officers exchanged a look, similar to the way a mechanic does with his colleagues when you ask him if there's a cheaper option than replacing the whole engine.

'I don't think there's much we can do for you.'

I was already shaking with fear and exhaustion and, as soon as the officer finished talking, I started to cry. 'I should have known,' I said, repeating the statement as I prepared to get up and go. This, as far as I could tell, was a typical case of cops not seeing past the transsexual issue. Dad suddenly swelled in his seat.

'You listen to me. My daughter has done everything she can to help this man who – it has been well documented – turns out to be a psychopathic drug addict. Look at her. Simon is six feet tall, built like an outhouse. If you don't do something, then he's going to kill her. And when that happens, because it will happen, that will be on you.'

'Look—' one of the officers began.

'No, you look. Either you or some other officer is going to help us. We're not leaving until you do. I don't think you realise how serious this is. If you send us away now and this man hurts one hair of my daughter's head, I will hold you entirely responsible.'

The two officers exchanged another glance. Then the older one said, 'Maybe Sandra can help you.' He turned to his colleague. 'She's had training in this, hasn't she?'

The other officer nodded and a few minutes later they said they'd call a detective specialised in domestic violence who might be able to help us.

Simon lied as usual. He turned on the charm and told the detective that I was making stuff up again, rolling his eyes, but Sandra wasn't fooled and managed to get him out of my flat and into temporary accommodation with promises of rehabilitation. There was nothing we could do about the child porn; it was my word against his and because my laptop had been left in public places, all Simon would have to do was say that a number of people could have had access to my laptop and the case would have been dismissed.

Simon made friends with three drug dealers at the hostel and they were all young, huge men. I started to receive abusive calls and once, after Simon had phoned me for a rant, he forgot to put the phone down and I heard them say what they were going to do to me. They were laughing when I heard him suddenly say, 'Fuck! She can still hear me.'

'You're in danger, girl,' I said to myself and I moved away, heading for a town as far as I could manage from Simon, into an emergency refuge, the kind of place where I'd worked. I wondered if I would ever be able to do that work again but I volunteered and soon found a job at a homeless shelter. That's where I met Pete, a fellow volunteer; the first person since Dad who talked to me with trust in his heart. I'd come so far, been through so much, and it was hard for me to open up. I felt that if I talked, then I would totally break down – I was still so damaged.

My life thus far with the people who were supposed to look after me had been a series of disasters – except for Dad – and when I tried to stand on my own, I'd found someone who abused me as badly as any other person in my life.

Pete gave me the time to talk to him at my own pace – slowly, piece by piece and over time. Joined by our love for the work we did and each other's passion, we fell in love.

Then Simon called one night at 3am, crying: 'I will always love you.'

'Well, I don't love you any more.'

The following day, Pete opened the front door to find police officers on the doorstep. They said that Simon had alleged that I'd been harassing him and his girlfriend. This time I didn't cry or panic. I told them that it was the other way around, that there were police records that proved it, records which explained that Simon was a jealous psychopath with a history of violence. With the help of a domestic violence outreach worker, we were able to convince the police to stop taking his calls seriously and to start threatening Simon with harassment charges.

But I was worried about Pete. 'I'm sorry,' I told him. 'You knew I came with baggage, I suppose, just not how much.'

Internally, my emotional self was fast crumbling into an ocean of fear and pain. I really, really wanted to be with this man, someone who'd understood me from the first moment. I was expecting to hear the words 'I can't handle this' or 'This is too much' and I even considered dumping him before it happened, I was that frightened of being abandoned. Pete took a long look into my eyes.

'I love you,' he said. 'And I'm here for you no matter what. We will get through this together. I want us to be together always.'

Pete and I live together as man and wife now. I still struggle with my many demons but they're shrinking and, if it ever gets too much, all I have to do is look at my favourite photograph. It is one of the three of us – Dad, Pete and me on the seafront, all smiling, relaxed – that's my family right there. With their love, I know I can be who I want to be.

AMANDA

I needed to be drunk constantly and when I was drunk I liked to shout and scream; just open my mouth and let rip. When that wasn't enough, I sharpened the plastic end of a Bic pen and pressed it into my arm. This happened most often during a blackout – I'd wake up the following morning without a single memory of the night before. I'd see the wounds on my arm and think, 'Oh no, not again.'

As for drugs, I literally used everything. I was only eighteen years old but craved total obliteration. It was as if an infinite and empty hole inside me needed filling with drugs. No matter what was in the medicine cabinet at friends' parents' houses, I'd crush it up and snort it all. This approach to getting high led me to casualty so often they called me The Frequent Flyer. I had not one but two out-of-body experiences, when I watched myself from above and knew I was dying. Two older boys who were into drugs, Trev and Cam, let me hang out with them because I was so crazy but even they tried to get me to slow down. I had a massive crush on Cam and, although we became a couple, we only ever hugged. They were decent guys and tried to do right by me, even though I shagged one of Cam's friends when we were still going out. I don't even know why. I couldn't sit still and be sober. It was impossible for me. I either had to be getting high or catatonic. At points in between I smashed everything I owned; I destroyed clothes, CDs, make-up, mirrors, everything. The only thing I owned I couldn't smash was a can of hairspray.

I went from Malcolm and Terry's B&B to a little bedsit paid for by the council, but the landlord threw me out when I jimmied the 50p electricity meter. I was terrified of being sober. If I was unlucky enough to come down, I became psychotic and had visions, seeing people and objects that weren't there. When a time came when I wasn't able to get hold of any drugs I got really scared and took myself to hospital. They put me in a psychiatric wing and, after many tests and a few days, I calmed down. The doctor told me I was badly anaemic and that there was something wrong with my hormones which would make it difficult for me to have children, although he said this might change if I stayed off drugs. Fat chance.

I received £2,000 compensation for the sexual abuse I suffered at the hands of Bill and I blew it in two days. When I finally turned eighteen, I was removed from care with a £100 'leaving care grant' and a duvet. I know the system wasn't perfect but when I look back at the chaotic mess of these last years of care, I can't but help wonder why I wasn't placed in long-term supervised care. Whenever someone had shown me patience and understanding, like Malcolm and Terry, I had shown the first glimmers of improvement. Instead, when I left care I asked for help and my social worker replied that I should be able to cope on my own.

So, cut loose from the one thing that might have protected me, I slept with every man who would have me, and took everyone's money, either in loans or stolen straight from their pockets. When I'd pissed everyone off so much that no one wanted to see me any more (or those who did want to see me wanted to hurt me), I ran away to London. I packed one bag and walked out. I arrived on the Strand, just by Trafalgar Square, aged eighteen without a penny to my name.

I was full of hate, ready to hate and be hated. I'd stopped taking hard drugs and opted for alcohol and weed – which I loved because when I smoked it with booze my mind went numb.

For some reason, in a rare moment of conscious awareness, I thought this might be the time to try and find my mum, move in with her and try and get my life under control. At that moment, though, I knew no one and nothing, so I slept on the street until a homeless man, seeing me shiver, gave me his sleeping bag and took me to the homeless charity London Connections. They were understanding and found me places in a few hostels until I got a live-in job working in a pub. It hadn't been so long ago that I'd been working three jobs and I was smart enough to say the right things. It helped that I was young, good-looking and a fast learner – a bit too fast, as I quickly learned how to steal drinks. For the moment, at least, I loved the job because it took care of my homelessness and cash problem in one fell swoop. The only catch was that, as an alcoholic, working in a pub was a dangerous occupation and I was soon fired for stealing booze, as well as thieving cash out of the till. But I was always able to find another live-in pub job and I carried on this way – a few months here and a few months there, until I was twenty-four years old and had become famous across London for being one to avoid when it came to offering bar work.

I ended up back at the Strand, living as much as I could in the slightly drier and warmer pedestrian tunnels of Charing Cross underground. I couldn't find another way out and, with no other option, I became one of those crazy people you see on the street talking to themselves, looking really dirty, with one small bag stuffed with my world's possessions.

The PTSD was still there and was only made worse by the homelessness – I was on constant alert, unless I managed to get hold of some weed for a good smoke that would take the edge off for a while. But it also made me paranoid and won me no friends at the ever-patient London Connections, where I whiled away the coldest days drinking tea and grabbing what food I could. When the centre was closed, I'd sit with anyone on the street, yelling abuse at the paedophiles preying on child runaways around the Strand and Charing Cross.

I didn't want to be housed; I didn't want to be indoors.

I knew nothing about the world but ranted against the government and made up a number of conspiracy theories. I also spent my days wandering around central London processing a great many strange thoughts about my life and the world in general, and I smoked a lot of drugs. I wanted to be permanently stoned. In the winter I drank to keep warm and, if it rained, I drank on the buses. If you're homeless in the winter and you get wet you're screwed, you'll never get dry again. It was a constant battle. I managed to survive, somehow, all on my own, for two years this way – two years that passed me by in a blur of streets, the occasional strange bed and the occasional beating carried out by some of the more dangerous members of the homeless community, which seemed to be divided into those who thought they'd figured out how to exist in the confusing pointlessness of life by sitting on the street and drinking the days away, and those who were on the street because they were just too horrible to exist in any version of the normal world, having messed up every last chance going through cruel violence. I felt like Travis Bickle, Robert De Niro's character in *Taxi Driver*, looking from an outside place at all the mess humans had made of the world, something I was a product of. I just couldn't understand it. What was the point of it all? What could I do about it? All these people, waking up, eating breakfast, going to work where they made money to put in the bank. And for what? What good did any of it do? Couldn't they see the pointlessness and misery of life? What was in their mind that wasn't in mine that allowed them to do this? I just wanted to be out of it – living in the present moment where my mind was too addled to think about the future and couldn't even consider looking back at my past.

Eventually, faced with a third winter on the streets, I took a chance when a doctor was in London Connections, braving the strange sicknesses of the street people, and told him I was vulnerable – that the streets were no place for an attractive young woman like me. He could do nothing but agree and he helped me get a flat – although I had to spend almost a year waiting in a series of foul, depressing B&B rooms across London first.

Once I was finally presented with a flat in a block in the middle of a patch of no-man's land in Mile End (a yellow police 'murder board' was the first thing I saw when I stepped out of the underground station), just beyond London's East End, I didn't know what to do with it. It came unfurnished, apart from a mattress on the floor, and that was how I lived in it. I'd never settled anywhere for any length of time. Furnishings and possessions meant nothing to me. I had no idea how and where, or why, one filled one's home with things.

I needed someone to talk to, so I asked the doctor to help with getting me therapy. He sent me to a place on the other side of town where I looked at a woman who looked at me. She reminded me of Celia and we didn't say much to one another, until we got on to the subject of social services and that got me fired up. Suddenly I poured out everything that had happened to me and why social services had messed up. She said I might have a case to sue them and so I contacted social services, asking for my files. They replied that they were missing.

I still smoked weed and ended up falling in love with the dealer who sold it to me, a tall man with long, black hair called Russell. I was obsessed with him and thought if we could have babies then that would mean we'd have to be together, to live as a family and that everything would be all right. It felt as though my body was screaming at me to get pregnant but I had fertility issues and so I asked my doctor if he could help. A few days before I was due to go into hospital to have an 'exploratory operation', I received a letter from social services. They'd found my files. A whole load of boxes had been found in the basement during a building move. Nice to know they were taking such good care of them.

On the day of the operation, I started to shake with terror. The nurses tried to reassure me, that it was just routine and that everything would be fine.

'I can't do this,' I said when a doctor brought me the premeds. 'I've never had an operation in my life. I just can't face it. Sorry.'

I left, deciding that I would first sort out my case with social services. In order to support myself and my addiction, I'd started shoplifting and found I was pretty good at it. I stole to order, taking requests from a number of West End brothels. All I needed was about £50 per day for weed, booze, smokes and food, but I made lots more and gave it all to Russell, who always seemed to be in need of cash. Social services had provided me with a support worker who was younger than me and I ended up giving *her* advice. Even though my flat had no bed, even though I hadn't cleaned the toilet for two years, and even though my house was full of suspiciously large amounts of new-looking clothes (some with the security tags still on them) and other items, as well as piles of poorly concealed drugs debris, she didn't challenge me on anything.

My relationship with Russell was really unusual, although I didn't realise this at the time. I was obsessed with Russell but he knew nothing about me; I just didn't think to tell him and he wasn't the kind of guy to ask. I didn't really have friends, as such, just acquaintances. My 'best acquaintance' was a prostitute.

I shoplifted from the same M&S store every single day and never got caught. I took my pick from the shops on Oxford Street. Either I was very good or the security guards just didn't care. I stole handbags, shoes, bangles, earrings, coats – anything I wanted, I nicked. I stole so much I couldn't get rid of it all. My flat was full of nicked gear, unworn, unused and with all the labels still attached. The retail value must have run into tens of thousands of pounds. Getting all this stuff was therapy for me. I was helping myself to everything I'd never had. I knew what I was doing was wrong and that I couldn't go on forever, and I told myself that when I got caught I'd have to stop. I certainly didn't want to go to prison. One of my other haunts was Brent Cross shopping centre in north London. I was leaving with bags full of stolen clothes when I decided to stop off at good old M&S. I spotted a large rack of lamb. It looked good and, although this wasn't something I'd ever stolen before (I certainly didn't know how to cook it), I grabbed one and was outside when a uniformed man took hold of my arm and asked to take a look in my bag. Apparently there'd been a run of thefts from the meat counter and they'd placed a permanent watch over it. I escaped prison with a twelve-month conditional discharge and no fine.

One of my best acquaintances, Rita, was a functioning alcoholic who'd grown up in care. She owned a hot dog and burger van that she parked on London's South Bank. She paid me £15 a day to sit with her, to keep her company and watch her van when she needed to pop out for a drink. One of her friends was a prostitute who was always flashing her money. 'It's not a bad way to make a living,' she told me as we started to hang out together. 'It's all right.'

She took me to a place in Frith Street in Soho, some rooms above a cab office. I gave my body to twenty men a day and made a small fortune, most of which I gave to Russell. Having the money made me feel powerful and I loved the fact that Russell was so grateful for it. I had no idea what he did with it all. I didn't care; I was addicted to him. It was like a drug for me. Every now and then I'd wake up feeling awful and couldn't work. I'd just lie in bed and, morose, I'd stab myself in the arms and legs with a sharpened Bic. I coped with the never-ending stream of men by putting myself in a different mental place, zoning out so I was outside the room and would come to when it was over – I preferred it when men came with drugs to share, that made it much easier to escape. All the shagging kept me very fit and I sometimes incorporated exercises into the sex, like stomach crunches while in the missionary position. I don't think any of the men knew; no one ever said anything.

Two old French ladies ran the brothel; they liked to joke that we'd put their kids through the finest private schools and universities in England. I was earning hundreds of pounds every day but my flat was still empty and the gas was cut off. What money I didn't give to Russell I spent on £400 dresses and never even thought about wearing them. I just looked at them.

There wasn't a single man who paid me for sex that I would ever have chosen to sleep with outside of the job. A barrister demanded sex without a condom. I said no.

'I'll pay you one thousand pounds.'

I thought he must have AIDS but I still did it.

There was only one guy – big and fat with mad, darting eyes and a loopy grin – who was so far gone, mentally speaking, that I thought he might actually be a psycho looking for his next victim. But, luckily for me, he only wanted to perform the most degrading acts imaginable – well, beyond most people's imaginations.

Most weren't weirdos; they were just ordinary men who were, for whatever reason, unable to connect emotionally with women. A few treated me like their mum. To begin with I put on an act and played along, but after a while I started to lose interest and fall apart. I couldn't play the part any more. I started to turn the strange ones and the mummy's boys away.

I don't know if the job had much to do with it but I lost interest in Russell. There was nowhere for our relationship to go. I didn't want to talk to him about myself but I liked the fact he was so happy when I gave him money. He was the first person to respond positively to my presence and I liked that. But eventually he seemed to take the money for granted, started to ask for it and it killed whatever it was in me that wanted to be with him. When I stopped going to see him he made no effort to come and see me.

The recession hit at around the same time and business took a sudden dive, leading the madams to get snappy (no doubt the school and university bills were mounting up) and I snapped back. One of the madams left the front door open in winter – there were only small electric heaters in the rooms. I only bothered to wear underwear while I was at work all day and I couldn't understand why I was feeling so cold. When I found out, I lost it and fell into a rage. I told them where to get off, stormed out of the door and never went back.

To make money to survive I started to sell my stolen clothes collection. It lasted three months. As my collection started to dwindle, I wondered what my next move should be. I was scared to decide. It wasn't as if any of my decisions had made much sense so far in my life. I thought about doing something positive, something that was good for me, and decided to try and stop all drugs.

But I wasn't sure how. Each day I looked at my clothes collection and each day there was a little less. I'd sit in front of it in my otherwise empty flat, staring at it, never worn, smoking weed and cigarettes. The days seemed to go on and on, blurring into a depressing mess. I just wanted to be a person like other people. How did they manage? What did they do? I had a suicide note I'd written months before but I had no idea who was going to read it, or why, let alone what the point of it was.

I chanced upon a Narcotics Anonymous meeting that was taking place near me and I went along, but it was awful. The whole evening was spent on one self-indulgent woman who did nothing but sob and moan. Then, on a day when I felt particularly hyper, I went to my local Mental Health Unit in a nondescript NHS building in Bethnal Green Road. My plan was to walk up to the front desk and ask them to 'make me normal' and see what happened. It was closed. But then I saw some people walking down some stairs into the basement. There was a Narcotics Anonymous meeting happening right there. I walked in the meeting and suddenly got it. I identified for the first time. My recovery had begun. It wasn't – and isn't – easy. I had some relapses at first, before I got help at a day programme.

They helped me deal with my addiction by helping me understand what friendship and love are. These were things I'd never had and didn't understand but I'm learning about them now.

Sometimes I think of that little girl, all those years ago, who, despite everything, believed in God – which is another way of saying she was full of hope for life. To this day, I can't get over how I found that meeting at exactly the right moment. In the end, I committed as much to NA as I had to drugs. It brought me love, friendship and understanding and, two years on, with the help of those friends, I'm still clean and even going to college. Every day is a battle. There's a lot I don't understand, and my interactions and emotions are often off kilter, compared to people who've had a relatively normal life, but I'm where I need to be. And now, because I have found love and friendship, I can bear the future and endure my past. Just about. I want to use my experiences to help people in my position, to use the tale of my life as a warning to others, and to make it clear that there is help and that, sometimes, the best people to help are the ones who've been through something similar to you.

TINA

They used a court order to force me go to a day programme, to get off the drugs. It was part of the care plan so that I could see my children, and perhaps work towards getting them back. I was allowed contact ninety minutes each week and this was the only time I was alive.

When I dragged myself to the clinic, I made sure I had plenty of speed in my pocket. I kept asking to be excused so I could go to the loo for a top-up. After what must have been the fifth time, someone cleared their throat loudly as I reached the doorway. I turned and saw Mandy, the manager.

'Need a toilet break again, Tina?'

Bitch, I thought, but smiled like butter wouldn't melt.

'Weak bladder, smaller than a tangerine.'

'All right, then. Well, when you come back, you can talk for a bit – and a bit faster no doubt.'

And a few minutes after I got back, seeing I was fidgety, Mandy said: 'Why don't you have another toilet break, take some more drugs and then we can have a chat about it, OK?'

When it came time for my hair strand test, the scientist included with his report a statement that said he'd never performed a test that yielded a result this high, and he'd been testing for fifteen years.

'Mary told me she thought there was more to you but that doesn't seem to be the case.' Mandy, who was a short, thin woman in her fifties, was a good judge of character and knew how to sting me into action.

My response to that statement was to say: 'How dare you?'

'Prove me wrong, then.'

'How?'

'Come with me. Get an A4 bit of paper, some coloured cards, scissors and coloured pens.'

'What is this, playschool?'

'Maybe. Now, cut out seven circles from seven different bits of card.'

'Where's this going?'

'Shut your gob for five minutes, do it and then we'll see.'

Once that was done Mandy said, 'Write Monday on this one.'

'Oh, let me guess, Tuesday on the next, Wednesday on the next.'

'Oh, you're not so bad, then.'

I didn't say it but I'm certain my expression read: 'I really hate you.'

'OK. I've done it.'

'On Monday leave it whole.'

'Yes, Mandy.'

'On Tuesday cut out a little triangle. And Wednesday another triangle. And keep going through the week, until there's nothing left on Sunday. That's how you're going to reduce your intake of speed. By Sunday you will take nothing. Only if you dare to take up the challenge. You up for it?'

'All right then, I will.' I was terrified but also my stubborn personality was worrying that I was going to lose face unless I did this. I rang Julie, my step-mum.

'Can I come and stay for a few days, please? I'm reducing my drug intake with the day centre people.'

She agreed. I think she knew that I'd never take drugs in my dad's house – but if I was in my home then I would. I always believed in the idea that if you're in someone else's home you play by their rules.

So I went, stayed and by Sunday I had done it. My body was aching like I had arthritis in every joint and flu to go with it.

Mandy had warned me. 'Next week you won't want to come in here and you will hate me even more. I don't care what you have to do and how you do it, but you get your arse in here.'

On Monday, Dad woke me with a cup of tea. 'Morning, mate.'

'Fuck your cup of tea,' I moaned. 'And fuck off yourself.'

'I beg your pardon?'

'Do I have to say it again?'

Even though I was under the duvet, I could sense Dad drawing himself up to his full height. 'You have two seconds to get out of that bed before I drag you out because I will dress you if I have to and you will be going.'

I poked my head out, looked at him and growled, 'Whatever.' Something told me that he meant it and I knew I was too weak to resist. He drove me over to the centre, me calling him every name under the sun on the way. He just sat there and took it. Once we arrived, I crawled up the stairs and pressed the buzzer.

Mandy took one look at me and knew I'd done it.

'We don't have to talk about anything right now and I appreciate you've got yourself here. If you go into the main room, you'll see a pile of giant bean bags in the corner; go over there and curl up.'

Withdrawal is a good word because that's what had to happen. I had to withdraw to recover. The hardest thing of all was not seeing my children because I was too sick, too weak. I knew, though, that I didn't have a snowball's chance in hell of having them back again unless I made this sacrifice.

For two weeks, Dad woke me, drove me in and I collapsed on the bean bags. Mandy had bent the rules to make this happen. She just explained to other people that this was my space, that I needed it, that I was doing something very difficult and to give me room.

Gradually the sickness gave way to fatigue and I slept all day until, two weeks in, I asked if I could sit in for the check-in, a meeting where everyone discussed how they were getting on.

Mandy couldn't keep the delight out of her voice. 'Yes, of course, yes!'

By lunchtime I had run out of steam and had curled up again. Three months later I was still sleeping in the day but they gave me another drugs test. The day it came back, Mandy took me to one side.

'I am pleased to tell you, young lady, that it's clear.'

I framed the damn thing and put it on my wall. It took five months before I could go a whole day without sleeping and before my body stopped feeling like it had been hit by a train.

The next piece of torture I had to endure was months of court cases in different buildings across the county. I still saw my children once a week. They were together and Sophie and Emily had accepted that Mummy wasn't well, while Angie was too young to know what was going on. I have to say, as much as I wanted to hate the foster family for being part of the system that took my kids, I had to admire them for the wonderful job they were doing. And, as I came off the drugs, my children looked more beautiful, happier, and more full of life than I'd ever seen them. As the speed left my system, they came into focus.

'Can we come home now?' Sophie asked when I explained how I was feeling much better.

I also took the time to visit Mum's grave, to talk to her about the mess I'd got myself into. I wept as I wished Dad had never done what he'd done. But I also told Mum that I forgave him and he had since tried to do right by us and I knew he felt tremendous guilt every day. And, of course, I promised her that my grandchildren would be back with me one day soon.

And then came the day when I stood in the court, with Gareth the guardian and Mary the social worker either side of me, and this time I was conscious and I understood everything that was happening. The judge told me the kids could, after a week of preparation, come home.

The following week they came for dinner every day

and by the weekend they were back – in a spotless house with sheets on all the beds and not the slightest speck of dust anywhere.

The feeling was both wonderful and scary – I was sober and now I had to be a 'real mum', while social services kept a close eye on me. But I knew I could do this. We were happy, the children were so excited to be back, excited to see the new me – a me that Sophie could remember from when Mum was still alive. We were a proper little family.

Three days after my kids came home, it was my brother's birthday and, with a party to be had, this seemed like a good time to get some new outfits for the girls. I now understood when people who have been through hellish experiences say every day is a blessing.

For everyone else in town hitting the shops, it was just a typical day; kids fooling around, fed-up fathers weighed down by shopping, screaming toddlers, charity collectors shaking their pots, hungover checkout girls and the cries of the people working the market stalls trying to shift the last of their fruit. I was in heaven. I was with my family, whole again and clean to boot. I had recently turned thirty and felt like this was truly a new beginning. Mum would have been proud and I felt like she was shining down on us at that moment.

As we drove back with Julie, I could see the column of smoke several streets away. When we turned into my street, it was like a crime scene with fire engines, ambulances, police and a coroner's van.

The fire was in my house. I threw up in the garden.

'This cannot be happening,' was all I could manage to say.

'We have to tell social services,' Julie said.

Then the police came and asked to talk to me – at the station.

'But what about my kids?'

'Sorry but you have to come with us.' It was soon clear that they suspected I was to blame. They thought I was an arsonist. I had to strip off all my clothes and put on a paper boiler suit. Hours later, I pleaded with them: 'I don't know where my kids are. My house has just burned down. Give me a break. Can't we do this later?'

They interviewed me regardless. The interviewing detective, a chubby, middle-aged man who looked about as bright as a dark room, said: 'An eyewitness saw you leaving the scene of the crime.'

I looked at him like he was mad. 'I live there. It is – was – my home. I was leaving with my children.'

At 9pm the fire service called to say the fire wasn't deliberate, it was down to faulty wiring.

I don't know how I kept my cool as the detective said, 'We have to make sure.'

All I had left were the clothes I was wearing, my handbag and a mobile phone.

The children stayed with their cousins that night. Because it was so late and they were already in bed, I went to Dad's, which was nearest to the police station and the only family home with a spare bed. The next day, waking up to this fresh nightmare, I felt a little less blessed, I have to admit. At 9am my phone rang. It was someone from social services. 'We're taking your children back today.'

'What?'

'They weren't kept in your care overnight.'

I put them on speaker so Julie could tell them that she made the decision after the house burned down and I had to go with the police. 'Tina wasn't there, the police took her, so I had to decide. I called to let you know what had happened. If there was something wrong you could have told us then.'

'I'm sorry. You have to get the children and tell them they're going back to live in foster care again.'

They reasoned that my house was either burned down by someone who was out to get me, or I started it accidentally, in which case I wasn't a safe mum, and the fact that a fire could burn down my house suggested I wasn't taking good care of the kids.

'Mum?' Sophie asked. 'What's going on?' Having to explain that they were going away again, back to the foster family, was so hard. I said it was because of the fire, until I had somewhere else to live. To let my kids go once was hard, to do so a second time, and this time through no fault of my own, was almost impossible to bear.

I had to go to court to fight social services, who initially claimed that they should be adopted. That battle I won and Sophie was allowed to stay with her step-gran and granddad, but Emily and Angie would stay with the foster carers.

A few weeks later, I was in town just after sorting out a flat, when I saw Liam, standing outside the pub he managed, having a smoke. I stopped.

'How's things?' he asked.

'Not that great, to be honest.'

'Yeah, you look like you could use some cheering up. How about it?'

'How about what?'

'I'll take you to the pictures tonight.'

'As long as it's not some nonsense with Jean-Claude van Damme.'

'You choose the film.'

I hadn't realised how much I needed to be close to someone and a pleasant evening at the pictures was followed by a passionate night in Liam's flat above the pub.

A few weeks later, I took a pregnancy test and, sure enough, I was going to have another child. This time I wanted to make sure I did everything properly and so I called social services to let them know and that I was planning to keep the baby.

'And what about the father?'

'Not interested.' And that was most certainly true. I never saw Liam again after that.

Social services sent me a lovely lady, Nikki, who I saw regularly, and everything was going just fine until Julie's son, my half-brother, died from a heroin overdose when I was eight months pregnant. He was in his early twenties and had fallen in with a bad crowd after leaving school, although no one knew he was injecting heroin. It was one of those events when you add up the parts afterwards and wonder how you could have been so stupid.

It was a shock coming home after the funeral, from being with lots of people and then alone again in the new, bare flat. I had time on my hands and that feeling of mental paralysis started to creep in. I picked up the phone, called my contact and took three grammes of speed all in one go. As soon as I'd taken it I thought: 'Oh my God, what have I done?'

Nothing I could do about it now, though. I was up for three days straight.

'Never again,' I told myself, and I knew this time I meant it. I've never touched another drug since.

A few days after the speed incident, Nikki the social worker called me up.

'Are you available to come in?'

'Why?'

'I'd like you to come in and have a chat with my manager.'

'Why?'

'Please, Tina, this isn't my doing. I know you've been going through a really hard time, but you have to come in.'

Even though she'd just buried her son, Julie drove me down to social services and came in to give me support. I didn't much like the look of the social work manager. By the end of the meeting, I hated him. It was as if he'd been sent to make my life difficult. Because my half-brother had died the way he had, they decided to look into my case again and change all the rules.

He ordered me into a mother and baby placement – as soon as I had my baby we would have to live with a foster family together for three months. If I didn't do it, then the baby would be removed.

'But I've just buried my brother and I'm about to give birth. I need to be near my family.'

'I've made up my mind. The order has been given.'

'How is this going to work with Sophie? She's a teenager now, she needs me.'

'As long as Julie is OK to let Sophie live with her, that's fine with us and we will provide money for train tickets so she can come and see you.'

We were both reeling when we left the office. I called Nikki, who apologised, adding: 'I completely disagree with it but he's the manager, he's made up his mind and there's nothing I can do.'

As I prepared to give birth, I packed my bags, knowing I wouldn't be going home after the hospital. I was expecting Nikki to be there but I didn't know that she'd fought with her manager over my case and then, when she turned in her notice, he told her to leave immediately. Instead, I was joined by someone I didn't know, who described me as 'combative' because I wasn't happy that no one had thought to tell me the social worker I knew and trusted wouldn't be with me at one of the most important and difficult moments of my life.

Sylvie was born perfect and beautiful and, after a week in hospital, we were driven down to a coastal town in Norfolk – wide, windswept landscapes, big skies and grey seas – to meet Mark and Sue, our foster parents. I was so nervous about meeting them that I thought I might be sick. So much depended on how we got on, what life would be like for the next few months and whether I'd be able to keep Sylvie. I didn't much like the idea that I was about to invade someone else's family and that I'd be living in a glass house, with everyone watching my every move.

Mark and Sue were retired and in their early sixties.

Sue welcomed me with a warm smile. 'You're here 'cause shit happens,' she said. 'And if I can help, then, that's what I'd like to do.' She then added, 'Just a couple of things I need to make sure you understand: I love babies but I do not wash babies' bottoms; I do not do your washing; I do not clean the bathroom up after you; I will not hoover; nor, under any circumstances, will I change nappies.'

By now I was laughing, Sue had a way of speaking that made you smile. I knew she meant it and I said I understood and that I'd give them no trouble.

'Time will tell, girl,' she said. 'I'll show you your room.'

I loved them both right from the start. They made me feel that I belonged. It wasn't like they were doing 'a job'. They were the loveliest, liveliest sixty-somethings you could ever hope to meet. They embraced me into their family. I thought their children might be spoiled brats but, while they wanted for nothing, they were wonderful. Their daughter, Donna, had a horse and soon I was going down with her to the stables each morning. I loved the company of the horse, the love it seemed to show Donna and the peace and quiet of the countryside.

Mark and Sue became, after Mum, and along with Dad and Julie, the most important people in my life. I cried with joy when their eldest son, who had left home, asked me to be a bridesmaid at his wedding. No one in my family was married, let alone had had a traditional wedding, and the amount of love in the room took me by surprise; it was emotional but in the most wonderful way.

Not long after the wedding, social services called. They wanted me to come in for a hair strand test to make sure I'd not been using. The result would go in my file and form part of the decisions made at the end of the placement.

'No problem,' I said, because I hadn't been using. It was only when I hung up that it hit me. I had used. I'd taken three grammes just over four months ago. It would show up on the hair strand test.

Everything had been going so well. I'd been a good mum, Mark and Sue kept saying how wonderful I was as a mother, that I was a natural – and I felt as though I was. I still saw Emily and Angie once a week and loved them so much. I wrestled with the thought of telling them that the test could come back with a tiny positive result, explain to them it was a one-off, but eventually decided against it. One wrong step was enough to break my agreement with social services and for them to take Sylvie away.

I travelled on the train to take the test at a lab, where a scientist plucked a random selection of hairs, popped them in a plastic bag, sealed and labelled it. I signed some paper-work and then she placed my sample in with a load of others in a drawer.

It was at this point that I developed a sudden and nasty 'cough' and it wasn't long before the scientist offered me a glass of water. I nodded my thanks in between coughs and, as soon as she went to get it, I reached into the drawer, pulled out my sample and stuffed it down my jeans. She returned with the glass of water and didn't realise anything was amiss. I necked the water then got up to go. Once I was on the train and it was travelling at high speed between stations I took out my sample, tore it open and threw it away out of the window.

I just hoped they'd forget about it and, after a couple of weeks, I thought they had. We went on a camping holiday, something else I'd never done before but, again, I loved every moment; open skies, cooking and eating outdoors, other people's kids running around in the day, peace and quiet at night – everyone was so friendly. It was only on the drive home that I fell quiet with a sense of foreboding.

'What's got into you?' Sue asked.

'Nothing, I'm fine,' I answered. 'Just sorry the holiday's over, that's all.'

The call came a few days later.

'That's funny,' Sue said, hanging up the phone. 'You'll never guess, the lab's only lost your results. You're going to have to do another one.'

'Seriously? Can you double-check? I don't want to have to go through all that again.'

Bless her, Sue checked and this time the scientist said my sample had been posted to the testing lab before 5p.m. on the day it was done. Only I knew she was lying. So, I had no choice but to do another one and pray that I was lucky, that the amount was so small the test wouldn't pick it up. There were tricks to get around the test, like bleaching one's hair, but that was actually forbidden as part of the agreement with social services. I pleaded, but was told I had to take one before the court was due to rule on my future.

So I went, had it done, left the office and cried all the way home. A few days later, the results arrived. I had tested 0.003 positive for amphetamine. They could tell I had taken exactly three grammes.

Sue started sobbing when she saw the results. The guardian of the court came to see me the next day.

'You know, I genuinely believed you. I believed you when you told me you were clean. I can't work with you any more because I don't know if I can believe anything you tell me.'

The first decision was delivered tenderly by a social worker, who must have dreaded this part of her job. 'I'm sorry, but you're going to have to go home this week without Sylvie.'

My heart broke again. The one thing that reassured me at least was that Mark and Sue would be looking after her until the court made a final decision. Sue was beside herself and even Mark choked up with tears when he tried to tell me how much he loved us both.

'You know she will be OK ,' he said. 'We love you both so much.' They gave me the strength to walk out of the door.

The court date arrived a few weeks later. It was just before Christmas. I'd had the same barrister throughout my time in court and he had seen how much I had changed and was extremely sympathetic but not hopeful. Then the judge sent the clerk in to talk to him. A minute later, he took me to a quiet corner.

'The judge would like you to know we can put you through a four-day hearing but he has read the reports and is planning to side with social services. He knows how hard it will be for you to endure four days of this and no matter what you tell him, the outcome based on the evidence presented to him will be the same. You can go through the hearing, or you can sign a statement that says you disagree with the decision and the judge will spare you the hearing and issue the adoption order for Sylvie, Emily and Angie.'

I nodded, unable to speak, tears already pouring.

The judge then asked to see me in his chambers. 'I wanted to thank you personally,' he said. 'I understand how difficult this must have been for you.'

I thought he couldn't possibly know, but I understood what he was trying to say.

That night Sue texted me, asking what had happened. I couldn't believe that social services hadn't told them already and it was left to me to say, in a text: 'I lost.'

I didn't get a response for hours – then Sue called: 'I am so sorry.'

I travelled down to see Sylvie every day with Mark and Sue before my visits were cut to three times a week for two weeks, once a week for three weeks and then – the final goodbye.

Before that day came, I wanted to meet Sylvie's adoptive parents. The social services said they'd have to check and luckily they actually wanted to meet me.

They already had a five-year-old boy. They'd adopted him when he was one and had wanted to meet his mum and, although she'd agreed, she didn't turn up on the day.

Before the meeting was due to take place Julie asked: 'Are you sure you want to do this?'

'If I don't, then I won't know if they're right for Sylvie. I'll start imagining all sorts of things about them, that they're evil child abusers or something. The moment I see them, I'll know if they're right or wrong for Sylvie.'

We met in a private room in a social services building. Julie took me and we were both sobbing before we went in. We explained we needed a minute and it took me a little while to brace myself sufficiently. This, for me, was a major part of the impossible task of letting go of my perfect baby.

They were a young couple and both of them hugged me when they came into the room. They were lovely and down to earth; I knew they were right for Sylvie.

The husband said, 'We looked at lots of different children, waiting for the right one to come along, and then we saw your daughter.'

I managed to stay for about fifteen minutes, until it started to sink in that this man would be father to my daughter, that she would have no memory of me. All the things to come – walking, talking, school, boyfriends – these would belong to these people. I was overtaken by an overwhelming urge to leave. I had done what I needed to do and could at least rest easy in the sense that they would give Sylvie a great life. I got up.

'I have to go now,' I said quietly. 'Thank you very much for seeing me.'

Two weeks later I received a card in the post. It said: 'Dear Tina, Thanks so much for coming to meet us. Please take comfort in the fact that we will look after Sylvie with love in our hearts and we would like to stay in touch.'

They went above and beyond the call of duty. They wrote to me explaining how they became adopters, and how happy they were when social services accepted them.

I called Sue and told her all about them. 'They're all right, they are,' she said. 'Someone has been looking out for you and Sylvie, as far as they're concerned.'

In the run-up to saying goodbye, we made a photo album with all of us (I put a picture of Sylvie in a locket I wear every day) and a trinket box with letters from Sophie and me to give to Sylvie's adoptive parents.

Being in that foster placement with Mark and Sue is the reason I'm here today, sober and in one mental piece. How and why and what happened to me, and the results, well, I don't really look for an answer any more.

Mark and Sue changed my life for the better. They taught me patience, how to enjoy life, that it was OK to be sad and moan, to tell them your troubles. They made me realise that I can cope with anything, any situation without using, regardless of the outcome, good or bad.

I can live without using.

Maybe Sylvie will want to find me one day and I sure as hell don't want her to find a user, or a gravestone. I live for the day when she comes to find me and want to be the best person I can when that day happens.

If she doesn't want to find me then I'll know for a fact that she's happy where she is.

Mum was left with one of us until later in life, and that's how it's going to be for me. I still have Sophie and she had her own daughter not long after Sylvie departed. Although she had a boyfriend who loved her and stayed with her, Sophie needed me. She was so young and I helped her through some difficult and dark times after the birth before she came through it and now I'm delighted to see she's an amazing mum and I'm a damn good gran.

I may have lost my other children to adoption but we have all survived, and I feel as though we will one day be reunited, a family once more. There was a cycle that needed to be broken and I think I've managed that now. I'm clean and living a good life with my daughter and my granddaughter. I have letterbox contact with Sylvie, Emily and Angie.

I wouldn't wish what I went through on my worst enemy. That was a phrase my mum used to use and I think

I sound like her sometimes. She taught me so much in those few years we had together – and when I think of her now, when times are difficult, I invariably hear her telling me something I need to hear. She told me that you do not have to go through life as a martyr, but that lying and doing the wrong thing is so hard – exhausting, in fact. If you have faith, be honest, embrace life's ups and downs, then, when the time comes, when you have to make a choice, you will do the right thing.

ANGELIKA

My foster home was clean and warm; I had my own
shower and could help myself to food. The couple, Mark
and Judy, were both about fifty and lovely. I found it
really easy to socialise with them. They asked me lots of
questions without making it sound as though they were
being nosey – they were interested in what I had to say,
what I *thought*. It was strange at first; this wasn't a type of
conversation I was used to. I would wonder why Mark
and Judy, clever and successful people, cared about what
I thought, when they knew far more than me about
everything.

I was helped by their daughter Becca, who was more or
less my age. She had no trouble voicing her own opinions
and got me to join in – it was fun. Me and Becca got along
just fine; I really appreciated the fact that she was able to
share her parents with me. If they were my parents, I
wouldn't have wanted to share them with anyone because
they were so good.

One of the harder things to deal with was that Mark was a security guard. This scared me at first but he was so gentle and understanding that I quickly took to him, and saw him as a big softie. After I'd been with them for a couple of weeks, Mark came home a bit late and plonked himself down at the dinner table with his uniform still on. It was too formal. It felt wrong.

'I'm not eating dinner with you like that!' I said.

'Like what?' Mark asked.

'You're still in your work clothes; you're not on duty any more. You're supposed to be part of the family.'

'Fair enough,' Mark said, and he went and got changed. He never wore his uniform at the table again and I really appreciated that he listened to me.

The whole family showed me a way of looking at my life in a new way – to make plans, think of the future and how to manage my money. They took me on outings and, during the long drives, we discussed what I might do in the future. We came up with the idea of hairdressing and they helped me find a work placement with the local branch of a large chain.

I was also able to go and see my dad. I hadn't been home for months and, from the moment I saw the front door, I noticed that the house felt different, as though all the life had been sucked out of it. Dad gave me a long, lovely hug when he opened the door. It wasn't a home any more, though; none of us kids were screaming, arguing with one another, or laughing at cartoons. It was just a building with a sad, old man inside.

Mum had vanished again and had moved in with the father of her new baby. Dad was drinking, not like an alcoholic, but enough to worry me that he was depressed, as though he'd given up. He was lonely and felt like he'd lost everything. All he'd ever wanted was his family. He wanted to provide us with a secure and straightforward life, and he had failed. We were spread out, in different homes, in different towns, living separate lives.

I made sure I came back two or three times a week to check on him. I promised him we would be a family again, that this was just temporary, but I could tell he didn't believe me.

My foster parents also took me to see Davina and Stanny; we met at Burger King. Someone from social services had to be there and wrote everything down, which was really weird and made a lot of my conversation quite stilted. I wanted to talk about Dad but I didn't want to increase our chances of staying in foster care for any longer. As much as I liked Mark and Judy, I loved Dad and I wanted to be with him and help him. He needed us.

Stanny didn't seem to care. He said they'd hit the jack-pot. Their foster family was rich and they were getting everything they wanted – Nike trainers that cost £100, skateboards and all the latest PlayStation games, and they'd been on holiday to Spain.

'I'm worried about Dad,' I told Stanny when the social worker left to use the loo. 'He's drinking; I think he's depressed. He needs us back with him.'

Stanny looked down for a moment, then back at me. 'I'm happy now,' he said. 'Can't I just enjoy myself?'

He looked anything but happy. If I had to pick one word to describe him, it would have been angry. Maybe he was confused. I was certain that Stanny wanted to go home but his foster family had brainwashed him into wanting to stay with them, thanks to all the presents and the promise of a nice life ahead.

Sure enough, Stanny's anger soon burst out in the form of rage against his foster parents. He got into a shouting match with his foster mother and demanded to be moved. The social workers tried to persuade him to stay but Stanny insisted he didn't want to live there any more, so they moved him. Davina stayed.

It was wonderful that these foster parents wanted to show these broken-home kids a good time with lots of presents and holidays, but I think children need emotional support a lot more. There quickly comes a point where a new pair of trainers or a PlayStation game won't help.

Even though things had not gone well for us, nearly all the social workers I'd met had been fantastic. And then Gillian started turning up. She promised Dad that she would help him find a new house, a school for the kids and a job for him, but she did nothing and when Dad asked, Gillian told him: 'I'm not allowed to help you. You have to do it yourself.'

So Dad went and found a new job on his own. He saved some money and found a new house. He then went to court to try and get us back. There were two cases, first up was Davina and Stanny, and, although Dad was ready to fight for them, he was taken by surprise at an unexpected report from Gillian.

Gillian had paid Dad surprise visits. The house was usually clean and there was fruit on the table, nothing fancy but liveable. But Gillian made it sound as though Dad was an alcoholic. He did drink after we'd gone but who wouldn't in his position? He could have taken tranquillisers but he preferred to drink. In her reports, Gillian made it sound like Dad couldn't get through the day without a drink, which I knew wasn't true.

I kept asking about going home to Dad and when I was told that Gillian thought he had an alcohol problem I believed her, because all of our previous social workers had been so good. 'We're never going to be a family again,' I thought, and I became really angry. I withdrew from family life at my foster carers'. I was full of anger but I didn't know how to let it out. I couldn't sit still. I needed to do something to let it out.

So I ran away.

It started with a party. A house packed with young people. Music banging. Parents away. It only took me a few minutes to find what I'd been looking for: marijuana. The one thing that could make me feel better. I gratefully took a drag from the joint that was going around, and asked who was selling. A short, dark-haired boy, wearing dark glasses and an old army jacket, pointed me in the right direction.

'You want to find Ruben,' he said, trying to see down the hall. 'There he is. Tall, curly hair.'

'I see him, thanks,' I answered, quickly digging out my stash of pocket money to buy some.

Ruben was a bit older than the others. 'I'm not really a dealer,' he said; 'I just know someone and am selling it to friends.' We sat and shared a smoke together in one of the bedrooms. I felt better and better. 'Why couldn't it always be like this?' I wondered. We stayed there most of the night, as people came and went, joining us for a smoke and a chat, before heading off again. Then the boy with the army jacket showed up. 'Got any of that resin, Ruben?' Ruben nodded and took out a small black lump. I'd only smoked grass up until now. 'What's that?' I asked.

'Finest hash from the fields of Lebanon,' the short boy answered. Ruben made a joint and we smoked it. It was nice.

'What brings you here?' the short boy, whose name was Nathan, asked.

'This,' I said, holding up the joint.

'Amen to that.'

'And what brings you here?'

Ruben laughed. 'It's his parents' house we're currently trashing.'

'Aren't you worried you're going to get into trouble?'

'Worried? Me?' Nathan said. 'No chance. What are they going to do? Chuck me out on the street?'

The room started to lighten. Dawn was coming. To make the most of it, Nathan took us up to a roof terrace to see the sun come up. We had a nice view of some hills and, in the distance, the beginnings of London. We smoked and drank as the sky turned from grey to pink. Trippy music came from inside the house. 'Why couldn't it always be like this?' I asked myself again. Always at these moments, thoughts of my family crept in. My mum messing things up, my dad's failure to hold us together, Stanny falling apart, and now me. Was that all waiting for Davina, too?

I didn't go home that night. I stayed with Ruben and Nathan and helped them clean up after the party. I didn't go back the next night either and then, once Nathan's parents were due back, I met Ruben at another party and stayed out all night again and went home with Ruben in the daytime. He was at university and lived in a house with lots of other students, who all talked about their incomprehensible studies and all the parties they were going to. They made life sound so easy and I was jealous. Ruben had a computer, so I decided to have a look on Facebook. There was a post on my timeline from Mark, my foster carer, telling me off, proper Dad style, adding that I had been reported as a missing person and I needed to get in touch as soon as possible. I didn't like that at all. It made me angry. I couldn't see that he was worried sick and just wanted me back safe and sound, or at least to know, through Facebook, that I was OK. I wasn't prepared to do that. What future was there for me without my family? Better to leave now and spend as much time out of it as possible because there was nothing else to do. I quickly shut down the laptop – Ruben thought I was his age.

'I need to smoke a spliff most urgently,' I told him.

'Sorry, I've got nothing left. We've smoked ourselves clean out.'

'Can you get some more?'

He checked his pockets. 'Need some more cash, you got anything?'

I scraped together about £15; it was all I had left.

'Still not enough for an ounce. Let's see if Nathan can chip in.'

So we walked over to Nathan's house and that's where four police officers found me, practically unconscious, later that night. Mark had made sure every police officer in the county had a picture of me and, because he was a security guard, his workmates had pulled out all the stops for him.

When the cops brought me back to Mark and Judy's house, Gillian the social worker was there. Reality bites. Surrounded by cops, carers and busybodies, I was ready for my telling off but Mark and Judy took me to one side instead.

'It's your father,' Judy said.

Dad didn't think anything of it when he opened the door to the woman from the gas company. She was in uniform, had a clipboard and he waved her in. He'd been playing cards and drinking with a friend, Terry, who was in his sixties, and he left the woman to it and told her to show herself out.

Thirty minutes later there was another knock on the door. This time when Dad started to open it, it exploded inwards followed by two huge thugs who, slamming the door behind them, pushed Dad back into the kitchen, kicking and punching him as they went. Dad used to be able to fight but he was old now, smoked, drank and never exercised. The men had no mercy. Even when he was on the ground, they kicked him in the ribs, then the head, until he was barely conscious. His friend Terry was even older than Dad, and smaller. They punched him, even though he begged them not to, and said that he would be no trouble. They beat him to the floor, where they bound and gagged him. Terry could see Dad was in a bad way but there was nothing he could do as they dragged and threw him into the hall cupboard, which they then locked from the outside. The men trashed the house, tearing everything to shreds, taking their time to look for any secret stashes of cash. They took what little there was, as well as our passports and a little bit of jewellery.

Dad, dazed, tried to crawl out of the house – perhaps to call for help, perhaps simply to try and get away. The men were angry. Terry, trapped in the cupboard, could hear them shouting at Dad. He thought they sounded Romanian. They were angry that Dad didn't have more stuff for them to take. They wanted to know if he had money stashed somewhere. A lot of immigrants don't use bank accounts and prefer to keep money at home, especially if it's made off the books. But Dad didn't make much money and he'd just spent what he'd saved on a deposit for the new house and buying furnishings for us. That was Dad. He always wanted us to have everything. I don't know what Dad told them, if anything, Terry couldn't hear – but he did hear the sickening thump of the hammer they used to hit Dad on the back of the head as he lay helpless on the floor.

Terry was sitting on a chair by my father's bed. Terry looked awful. He was bandaged, stitched and one of his eyes was swollen shut. Dad looked a lot worse. He had tubes coming out of him. As I drew close, I didn't recognise him. He looked so utterly different from the man who came to the UK those few years ago. Apart from the breaks and bruises, his face was so sunken, pale and death-like. He had an enormous amount of bandages wrapped around his head and a special pillow was supporting his neck, lifting it off the bed, so the back of his skull wasn't touching anything.

How quickly it had all fallen apart. Everything was a result of Mum messing up. I leaned over Dad and told him

I loved him. 'We're going to be a family again, Papa. All of us together. I'm going to look after you; then we're going to fight to get Davina and Stanny back. I swear it will happen, Dad.'

He didn't move. I was worried he was in a coma, but the doctors said he was sleeping.

'How long will he have to stay here?' I asked.

'That depends. Let's see how he's doing when he wakes up.'

Our home looked like a scrapyard. There were holes in the walls the robbers had made trying to smash their way through with the hammer, which they then used to bludgeon my Dad. Plaster covered the floor. The banister was smashed and hanging free, doors were off their hinges and the kitchen was full of water from where they'd smashed the pipes. The cupboards were smashed and the floor was covered in broken plates – plates we'd never even got to use. I moved back in with Mark and Judy and was a new person. They'd treated me so kindly and I'd repaid them by turning into the same monster that brought me to them in the first place. I wanted to change for them, for Dad, to show them I was responsible, that I was becoming an adult. I just wish that Mum had done something similar. I don't know what had made her do the things she'd done, and behave the way she did. She'd told Dad she loved him and I couldn't understand how you could behave like that to someone you loved.

It took a while for Dad to get out of hospital but, as soon as he was fit, I asked to go home. When Gillian asked me why now I replied: 'I just feel like the time is right.' It took a few months but I started seeing Dad most days in the run-up and so I felt more than ready when the time was right. Dad had moved again after the burglary. He found it hard to live alone and was worried about it happening again. Once he had a job he paid to have an alarm installed and now we have bars on the windows and the best locks possible on the doors. It feels a bit over-whelming – a bit prison-like – but at least Dad can sleep at night. I still see Mark and Judy and they said they'll always be there for me, no matter what. I've continued with the hairdressing and we're still fighting to get Stanny and Davina home. We see them often and Mum comes with us sometimes. She's doing well with her new family now. I still love her. After all, she's my mum, despite what she's done. And I think that, perhaps, we're not so different. I mean, we look alike but we also think alike. We both get frightened by life and want to run away. But I want to break the cycle. Thanks to Mark and Judy; I think they've shown me how.

Actions that lead you to being taken into care take no time, but restoring normality afterwards can take years. If there's one thing I've learned, it's patience. And I've taught myself to stop and think twice before I make a bad deci-sion. I understand now that life is not about trying to be happy, not in the sense that I was trying to be happy before – through drugs and living in a bubble of parties – but about being with the ones you love. The people who you love through thick and thin, side-by-side.

SARAH

The council provided me with a tiny two-bedroom house in the town centre. It was lovely but it was just for me and Michael. Robbie had attended rehab and was having to give supervised daily urine samples. They were coming back clean and he kept this up until social services agreed that he could move in.

It seemed as though, at long last, I had achieved everything I could have wanted – until I caught Robbie shooting up speed in the kitchen.

'What are you doing; I thought you were clean?'

'Me, no, of course not, been buying clean piss to take into the clinic. No one actually watches you pee; it's easy. Look, you don't have to use, all right?'

So I did my best with Robbie either high or stealing to get high and made sure not a crumb of drugs or drug debris was anywhere when the social services came to visit. Dad wanted to see me on my nineteenth birthday so I went home and left Michael with my dad and step-mum while I went out clubbing with two friends from the old days.

Robbie didn't like that.

'You should be here with me. You didn't say what you were doing.'

'I did but you were out of it, you didn't listen. Then you were out all day. Leave me alone; I want to go to bed.'

'No, we need to talk about this. Have some speed, then you won't be tired and we can talk.'

I looked at the open paper wrap in Robbie's hand, at the white crystals twinkling under the lamplight for a long moment, and something inside me clicked. Everything, even Michael, was forgotten in that moment, as one part of my brain that wanted this drug had blanked out all other thought and was telling me to take it, that there was no reason not to, that I should just take the speed and talk to Robbie.

From that moment, I started using every day, as if I'd never been off it. Life was exactly the same as before. I stayed up all night. People, other junkies, started to come in and out of the house – people I didn't know but barely noticed. I tried to keep it away from Michael but how could I? I thought I was doing a good job – I was feeding and changing him as always. Everything, as far as I could see, was OK.

But the more I used, the less I saw, the more the fragile world I'd built started to crumble, descending into the chaos that always comes with drug abuse. I injected amphetamine until one day Robbie said he had nothing but heroin and so I took that – but only after Michael was asleep. That was as far as my reasoning went – I thought I was managing my drug use around my parenting but I was really managing my parenting around my drug use. I knew I'd proven myself to be a good mum when I wasn't using and I thought I could continue to be a good mum when I was using; that it was still me here, behind the drugs – nothing, least of all drugs, was going to stop me from loving my little boy.

At the same time, it didn't cross my mind to ask for help. Although I knew that I was doing something terribly wrong, asking for help or telling anyone official would have meant losing the flat and probably Michael. All I knew was that I had to hide it from the social workers – and my dad. I wouldn't answer the door when he came around, not unless I was alone with Michael and I'd been able to clean the flat of drug materials.

I thought I'd fooled social services, mainly because they never made an unannounced visit. Perhaps they didn't feel the need, because I'd done so well since the mother and baby placement, but I was nervous nonetheless when I was due to go back to court. Michael was under a child protection order and social services told me they were going to bring it down to something less, reduce the amount of supervision.

One of our regular visitors, a junkie called Simone, had lost her kids to social services and I asked her whether she thought there was a chance I'd lose Michael.

'Not a chance,' she said. 'Sounds to me like you've done everything right and they don't know anything.'

I asked Robbie if he would come with me.

'Nah, babe,' he said. 'It's nothing to worry about and I got to see a guy about some metal, make us some money, you know?' He smiled. 'Go on, you'll be fine, right?'

I'd arranged for a friend, someone who wasn't using, to sit with Michael while I went to court. Now I was really scared. Nineteen years old, full of the paranoia that extended drug use brings, that strange disconnect from spending so much time absent, mentally and physically, from the real world – and nothing was more real than a courtroom, full of educated people with real jobs.

Still, I told myself, just nod along to everything they say and I'll be out in no time. The funny thing was, I'd never had a drug test from the day Michael was born and they still thought Robbie wasn't using because, even though the social workers came to the house when he was high (with dilated pupils and, in every other way, looking like the typical junkie) they never challenged him. I really didn't pay attention to what was going on until the judge said I had to sign a document that said I wouldn't contest the Section 20 order.

Section 20(1) of the Children Act (1989) allows social services to take a child into its care when the child has been lost or abandoned, or there is no one taking parental responsibility for him, or that the person who has been taking care of him has been prevented in any way, for any length of time, from providing him with suitable accommodation or care.

Stunned, powerless, I was driven back to my house by the social worker. An empty car seat was in her back seat. Michael reached out for me when I arrived to pick him up and cried as I put him in the car seat, arms outstretched. And that was it. The social worker had hardly a word for me, not that I heard what she said. And then she drove off with Michael. I was left alone, in the middle of the street.

The idea that I might never see him again started to sink in. I didn't move for a long time after the car disappeared from view, until I heard a soft beep behind me; it was a car trying to get past.

Robbie wasn't home. No doubt he was doing the business to fulfil our demands for drugs, the demands that had caused me to lose Michael. I waited for him. He didn't ask what had happened, so I told him and he went ballistic. 'If you hadn't signed that document then they wouldn't have taken him!'

This is true. I later found out that Section 20 should only be used in good faith and that, if I'd objected, they wouldn't have taken Michael there and then. I got angry with social services but failed to see that this was absolutely the right thing to have done. I wonder now sometimes whether, deep down, some part of me knew this and conspired with the drug-addicted part of my brain to sign the document.

But at the time I was angry – angry with social services for tricking me (as I saw it), angry with Robbie for not being there and preventing them from taking Michael, and angry with myself for failing my son.

My solution was to launch into my drug addiction with new vigour – which increased my dependency on Robbie. My little house filled with more and more drug users until it became a drop-in centre of sorts for junkies, and was known throughout the town.

I was allowed to see Michael, now in the care of a foster family, every day, and I dragged myself down in between hits to be with him. His first birthday came and went, then Christmas.

I struggled to stay in the system. I showed up for a hair

strand test with freshly bleached hair. The social worker who was there took one look at me and said: 'OK, no more hair bleaching from now on.' She made me sign a contract to that effect. The test was negative. I told her I wasn't using but she knew. I just wouldn't ever admit it.

I went to London for a psychiatric evaluation where a man gently quizzed me about my family, whether anyone in my family had a history of mental illness, about my upbringing, relationships with my parents and how I got on at school and, finally, about being a mother and about what was happening to me now.

They were stupid questions, in a sense. I'd messed up, I'd lost my son because of it and I hated the situation and myself, but all I knew was drug abuse and addiction and I was totally dependent on Robbie for drugs. But, of course, I never admitted to drug use. To say so, I felt, would be the worst thing I could do.

Despite this, social services were doing all they could to get me on a path to having Michael at home again. I managed to pull myself together whenever I saw and spoke to social services, and I was allowed unsupervised visits with Michael at the foster family's home. On these days, I would only use a little bit, so I wouldn't look or behave like I was high. The worst thing would have been to slip into a heroin nod while looking after Michael. That would have been the end of everything.

Michael and I played beautifully. He was small for his age but had caught up a great deal and was normal in every way. He made me laugh and for those precious two hours I was with him, my world of horror faded, and my desire for drugs faded.

I was loved and gave love back.

He was an independent little fellow, fearless and determined to explore, and he loved to try and stand with me in front, kneeling, holding his hands as he bounced then fell on his bottom laughing before holding his arms up, asking for the same again; this was a great new game. He was curious, too, always pointing and making a noise as if to ask, 'What's that?' He loved a little wind-up box that played 'Row Your Boat' in a twinkly tune, as pictures rolled past on a little display. He once plucked off my sunglasses, as if to see me better, and then tried to put them on – he looked hilarious, of course, and so cute but, before I knew it, my time was up. He cried every time I had to leave but I knew it wouldn't last long if I didn't drag out the goodbye, so it was a quick hug, a peck on the cheek and I was out the door, into the darkness of my world that closed in on me during the bus ride home.

Social services' main concern was Robbie, who didn't bother checking in at the contact centre as they'd asked. He was considered high risk. If I'd been on my own then I'm sure things would have moved a lot faster but, as ever, I could not exist without Robbie. Robbie provided me with what I needed to live.

At home, the house decomposed around me. Robbie had a huge motorbike that he parked in the lounge. It was so heavy, it caused the floor to bend. He dismantled it and never got around to putting it back together again. Oil and petrol was left on the floor, tools and engine parts were strewn around the room, making it impossible to sit anywhere.

I no longer bothered to get out of bed. More and more people came and went every day. A couple of people even overdosed and ambulances were called when we couldn't get them into someone's car or a taxi. I just watched TV, blank-faced, not even seeing much of what I was 'watching', waiting for Robbie to turn up with the drugs. I'd look for comfort in his eyes. As long as they sparkled, I thought, then we would be OK, he would keep getting me drugs.

Eight people were sleeping in Michael's room. Someone broke the sink, then someone else fell on the toilet and cracked it. People started peeing in the bath and no one ever cleaned it. It was too hard even to keep myself clean. With fifteen people staying in the house, and all their fellow junkies and dealers visiting, the kitchen became unusable, the sink became blocked and then stank so badly I felt queasy every time I went near it, which wasn't often. I can remember a guy called Gary, with a shaven head and a little rat's tail hanging from the back, saying loudly that this place was a tip and he couldn't live here any more. If even the junkies were starting to find it too much, well that goes to show just how bad it was.

But I took more and more drugs to make sure I was numb to it all – the filth, the pain, the misery. And still Robbie kept bringing the drugs. I told myself I loved him; this disgusting old man was the only person who understood what I was going through. Then Robbie asked if we could go to see Michael together. I agreed and we stopped off on the way to shoot up some speed. It was weird being there with Robbie; he didn't actually seem that interested in his son after the initial hello. I didn't expect him to, never had really; I had always seen Michael as mine only.

It seems amazing now but no one seemed to spot the fact that we were high during these visits.

There came a point, I'm not sure how or when, when there were other court dates, dates that passed me by. I was dragging myself out of the squalor to see Michael but that was all I could do. I was just existing at that level, and I was not showing social services that I was going to change my life to get Michael back. It is best for the child to try and move things on as quickly as possible so their life can settle in stability – after giving the parent as much time as possible to change.

I'm sure social workers hate their job sometimes, perhaps never more so than when they have to tell a mother that she isn't going to be able to keep her child any more.

Imagine being told your children are going to be taken away from you forever (or at least until they're adults when they might, if you're lucky, decide to look you up, if you're still alive). If you don't have children then imagine your brother or sister being taken away to live with another family. And then, imagine losing your mother, as a child. There can't be many things worse to have to experience. And then, to know that this happened because your mum chose something else over you – or that something else was more important to her that forced you to be apart.

When I was told, I was high and the news only enhanced my stupor and my desire to have more heroin and amphetamine. I wanted my little boy, to be playing with him on the foster family's living room floor forever. But I couldn't live without Robbie and the drugs he provided me with.

I was offered the chance to meet his adoptive parents. I couldn't bring myself to do it. It was like rubbing salt in the wound, as far as I was concerned. I hated social workers by now. When the final week I could have contact with Michael came, I couldn't do it. I just didn't go. It was too hard, impossible to go in, to play and leave again – a peck on the cheek and then out of his life. It was just fractionally less unbearable to escape the dread of that final hug, to know that it had already passed.

And then I went to prison. Shoplifting. Possession. More shoplifting. More possession. It wasn't something that was going to go away and no matter how reluctant the Crown Prosecution Service is to overload the already crowded prison cells, it was only a matter of time. I was sent away for three months and upon my release I was offered the chance to go to drugs rehab. I took the chance but I wasn't fully committed. I just wanted to kick heroin, as I could see the physical effects it was having on me – and I found the sheer addictive nature of that particular drug exhausting. So I went, kicked heroin and, while I was there, I had a brief affair. We were both kicked out as relationships were against the rules. My new boyfriend ended up back in prison and I started hanging around with the same old crowd, sofa surfing when I was lucky, sleeping on crack house floors when I wasn't. This was when I ran into Robbie, who was living in a hostel for the homeless. We carried on like nothing had ever changed, same old, same old, except this time Robbie had found a lonely old lady with a big house who had started to take in street people. Her name was Martina and she was on some kind of personal mission to help the homeless. Robbie moved in and took over the house. People came and went as they pleased and, one day, I spotted someone who was obviously straight, sitting in the lounge talking to an addict who had gone into a heroin nod.

'I don't think he can hear you any more,' I said.

The man smiled and introduced himself as Jeff. He was from an outreach charity and he offered me the chance to get clean if I wanted. I was still using and, as usual when with Robbie, I didn't have to do much to get my fix, so I don't know why exactly, but I said yes, I would.

I left with Jeff and he got me into a place at a really nice centre, where Robbie had been sent before me. We continued to see each other all this time. I was still using and wasn't testing clean. The idea was to try and minimise the harm I was doing through reduction and control.

Life wasn't any different, though. I'd wake up, drink a few cans of Tennent's Super, then move on to some bottles of wine, before heading off to the local M&S to steal meat, sell it to a lady around the corner and go and score heroin. I had another court date for shoplifting and another prison sentence hovering over me.

I was in the hostel on my third Tennent's of the morning when a friend of mine said she was going to an NA meeting. She asked me if I'd like to come. It had worked for her, she said. 'I think you'll like it.' So I went.

Two days later, I stopped using.

I identified almost immediately with the people at NA. I was amazed at how similar their stories were. I had known nothing else but drug abuse for most of my life and it was only now that I saw how the drug had burned away whatever I had to offer to the world, 'one line at a time', as one of the other addicts put it.

I still saw Robbie, except now I saw him sober. When it was Valentine's Day, Robbie sent me a big card. Everyone saw it. One of the day centre workers asked me what I was up to and I said I was going to meet Robbie. The worker should have challenged me on that but he didn't and I went with a six-pack of energy drinks to meet Robbie in the park, who came with a six-pack of high-strength lager.

I didn't have much trouble stopping but I still liked to sit around with the same old crowd of addicts. I could identify with them, too. The real world was just too unreal for me. That was a land where social workers and outreach workers, lawyers, judges and police officers worked. It might as well have been another planet. Sometimes, other users, drunk or high, couldn't inject themselves, so I did it for them.

I just didn't have a concept of right or wrong with regard to drug use. It was just part of my everyday life. I wasn't using but other people were, so I helped them. It never occurred to me the danger I was putting myself in. I found out later that there'd been a case where a man had been jailed for manslaughter after injecting a friend who had subsequently died.

I hadn't slept with Robbie for many months. Our relationship had become platonic, as I had only relied upon him for money and drugs. Without drugs, our relationship, what there was of it, quickly decayed. Once I moved from the hostel into a house share with other former addicts preparing for life in the outside world, I made friends – friends who were clean, nice to talk to, who understood, and with whom I could identify. Suddenly, that was all I was interested in – how to survive and function in the normal world. When I told people about my life and my relationship with Robbie, they made it clear to me where I'd gone wrong and what it was still possible for me to achieve.

Three years on and I'm still clean. I have a job. I work for an outreach charity helping vulnerable young mothers like myself, women in danger of losing their babies, who are in the middle of assessments they don't understand, or even recognise for what they are.

Now, when I see it from the other side, as a professional, I sometimes have to stop myself from jumping back to my own experience with Michael. Michael was so young and it hurt so badly, but I know that the right decision was made. It's strange to be sitting in staff meetings now and to see how hard everyone is working to help the mother keep her child and how upset people get when they have to include something in their report which will probably convince a judge to order the child be taken into protective care and put up for adoption. These experiences bring back far more memories than I thought they would. It makes me feel very sad – for them and for me. We cry often, but we cry out of love and that, at least, is a good thing.

I've applied to see my social work files. I just want to see it all in black and white – I think I'll be able to understand now and accept the decision. Seeing the files is an important piece of closure for me. I know I'm not that person who lost her child. I was a good mother during the mother and baby placement and I know I could be a wonderful mother again, if I ever meet the right person and decide to try and have children.

I'm not tempted to use. What I find hard to deal with is being near people who are able to use drink and who can still get on with their lives. It doesn't feel fair but I know where that one drink will take me – it will lead to a needle in my arm in a matter of hours.

Now I think social services do an amazing job. They always put the child first and that's what counts. Any mother, no matter how messed up, will hopefully understand that one day. I think there could still be more support for mums who lose their children, though. I was left on my own and I wasn't able to process what had happened in a way that would have allowed me to go through a natural grieving process, a process that helps people to accept the unacceptable. Some other mums cope by having another baby, which is not the answer, by any means.

I think of Michael every day. Several times a day. I know that if he ever wants to find me, he will find a different person, the real me. I hope he can forgive me and I hope he will understand that, for some people, addiction is more powerful than any love you can give or be given.

PETE

I wake up angry. I'm in a hospital bed and in pain, so much pain. I am fastened to the bed with broad straps. I want to get out and smash my way out of this room. I try to sit up and vomit blood and a nurse comes. She looks frightened. I try to tell her I won't hurt her but the words won't come.

This happens over and over again over the next few days.

I try to tell the doctors that I don't want medical attention; that I have always dealt with pain myself and I will deal with it now. I want to fight my way out of here but there's no hope. I'm already in prison.

My legs are broken. I have an ugly scar on my shaved head with many stitches. I know some ribs are broken, I can feel them poking around inside me as I try to move. Some teeth are missing. My hands are broken. Fingers are broken.

Someone tells me I am lucky to be alive. I just stare at the ceiling.

The cops tell me that Dave is badly hurt but he will make it. They want to know what happened. I just stare at the ceiling. They tell me I am wanted for other crimes involving GBH. They have a witness. I need a lawyer, they tell me. They found no drugs and no other people at the scene but they are going to prosecute me for the other crimes. I stare at the ceiling. I wonder what happened to the men I hurt. The cops eventually go away.

It is night-time and I want a drink, a smoke, a hundred lines of coke and a thousand hits of heroin. They have drugs in hospital but I can't move. I have to get out.

A doctor comes.

'We ran some tests,' he says. 'Your stomach, bladder, liver and kidneys are in a bad way. I'm most concerned about your heart.' He tells me I'm lucky to be alive. I tell him he's not the first person to say that.

'If you use drugs again, you will die from them,' he tells me. 'Probably in just a few weeks.'

I want to tell him I could have told him that.

I started stealing swigs from Dad's golden booze when I was six years old. I'd top up what was missing with water. Eventually it got too much and he noticed, especially when I puked up one afternoon. He made me a glass of vinegar to drink.

A year later, in care, I was smoking dope with other kids I had met down at the local park. And then that's all I remember. Every day was about getting out of it. If it ended with me unconscious in a park or in my bed, then so much the better. I was arrested a few times. I joined in with car thieves, 'taking without consent', then vandalism, possession (for which they stuck me in a cell; they wanted to give me a scare but I was so far gone I slept through the whole thing and even the next morning was just a cosy soft bubble of stonedness). School was just a place to sleep or run from. I was arrested a few more times and then I ran away from everyone and everything.

Then came speed, crack and heroin.

And here I am, twenty-three years old and at death's door.

But I just stare at the ceiling.

The doctor talks about the medication I'm on to deal with the pain and my addiction, that it's a very fragile balance but that once I'm strong enough they're going to take the drugs that are helping me away.

I just stare at the ceiling.

The doctor leaves.

I wake up every night, my brain screaming the same thing. Feed me. Coke, smack, booze, dope, whizz, crack. I want it all. I'm sobering up and it scares me; it's the scariest thing I've ever been through. I vomit a lot. I walk with crutches. The breaks were only fractures, I'm told. I'm lucky but I'll have a limp unless I do physio. Fuck physio, I think. I stop sleeping. I shake and ache and puke and feel scared. I'm sick. I need something to fill the void in me. The fear, the pain, the thing that hurts so much and is missing. Every time I open my mouth to say something I vomit.

I look at myself in the mirror. I see a grey, old man. Bald, scarred, limping, missing teeth. Pale, saggy skin. I look at my eyes. I am twenty-three years old. I try to see myself by looking deep into my eyes. I just see two blue and white orbs. I don't see a person there. There is no one there. Nothing behind my eyes, just emptiness. I feel scared and want drugs. I don't know anything about this person looking back at me. I don't know who he is. I'm scared and want drugs but I can't. I'm helpless and I can't.

Remand first, then court, then prison. Three years for GBH. For something I can't even remember. Which is what I said. I was high. I don't remember. Diminished responsibility, my solicitor said. Sounds about right to me, I thought. But three years, said the judge.

Every night in my cell I was alone. With this person I did not know.

I soon got into trouble when someone tried to challenge my washing-up abilities and they ended up on their arse with a saucepan-shaped dent in their head.

I got left alone. Then someone came to see me. A charity. They came and saw prisoners who had no one, made sure we were all right, that we had proper representation, if we needed it. The person was a lady. Her name was Janet.

I told her I wasn't a good talker.

She asked me why I was there and I tried to explain about diminished responsibility.

She asked me if she could come back in a few days and I said sure.

It felt good talking.

There were drugs in prison but I knew no one and had no friends inside. I never found out what happened to Dave. If he was out, he never came to visit. If he was dead or in jail, no one thought to tell me about it and I didn't ask.

I wanted drugs but the doctor's words stayed with me. Dead in a couple of weeks. I don't know why I didn't want to die, but there was something in me that said no, hang on. Just another day.

Next time Janet came, we ended up talking about my dad. I'd never talked about him to anyone. No one had ever asked me and I don't volunteer information. I told Janet how he used to hit me and torture me. She was shocked.

'Yeah, but I rubbed him up the wrong way,' I said. 'I tried his patience.'

'So that makes it all right, does it? Do you think it's OK to beat and torture a small boy for his difficult behaviour?'

I had to admit she had me there. But I didn't say so. Something in me made it hard to reply, and I thought of Etta – the Danish girl, the only girl I'd ever been able to talk to. And that made my eyes go wet.

We talked the next week. I told Janet that this wasn't the life I'd hoped to have. But I didn't have a clue what other kind there was. I had never tried to change. I just did whatever I felt like whenever I felt like it, without a thought of the consequences for me or anyone else. If someone stepped up to me, I made them step down and that was all. I did not know how to talk to people. No one had ever really tried to talk to me, except for Etta, and that had only lasted just a little while.

Janet asked me whether I would change my life if I could.

Sure, but to what I didn't know. 'I am a criminal and a drug addict,' I told her. 'I don't know anything else.'

She said she wasn't surprised. She said she might be able to get me into a programme that helps people like me.

'Will it get me out of here?'

'It might help get you out sooner,' she said.

There were activities for prisoners and I discovered I was good at metalwork. I made Janet a gift. A human figure. I saw it as me, crouching, with head lowered, one hand on the ground and one hand out to the side balancing, as if having landed from a great height. Bottoming Out, I called it.

I smoked a lot of cigarettes and drank a lot of coffee. They had their own little rushes that I liked.

I learned a great deal about who this person I am is while I was in prison. I hate what I've become. I hate that my humanity is defined by what is in the bottle, pipe and wrap. Drugs made me. They killed whatever was in me, whatever I could have become before I started taking them. And I hate my dad for killing whatever I might have been before that. The drugs had taken my personality and they were killing me physically. I am alone, so alone. When I am with people, I am alone. I can't connect, I can't relate and I can't understand. I don't feel what other people feel. And I can't stand it. This is what the drugs gave me. They filled that hole of loneliness. I want to understand people but I hate them because I can't understand them. I want someone to tell me it's going to be all right, that I'm not a worthless piece of shit, that I'm a person just like them. I have no one. Never had, except for Etta. And the thought of what I might have had with her, and what she might have given me, kills me. I doubt if she even remembers who I am. When I wake in the night, wanting drugs, after having the addict's dream, crying for help, asking for Etta, or someone who can give something like she could, there is no one and I am alone.

This is what goes through my mind while I'm in prison, after talking to Janet and, later, when I'm in therapy. I want to communicate but I don't know how. They ask me how I feel. Like shit. But I can't explain. The words don't come. Admission is weakness.

But if you don't admit to your weakness then no one can know you. And you will be alone.

I don't want to be alone.

Ah, so you don't want to be alone. You'd like to have a friend.

I can't speak, something is squeezing my throat. But that's it, I do. I want a friend. I want someone who can trust me, help me, love me. It feels like it's the only thing I've ever wanted. I am going to die alone.

I want to run, I want to smash things up, I want to hurt myself and I want to take drugs. I say it out loud and tears sting my face, and I weep. I cannot live like this any more, I say. I should just die. That's payback for all the people I've hurt. The men I stabbed. The things I smashed. All the things I did that hurt people in more ways than I know. I am nearly dead. My mind is something I do not know. I genuinely do not know who I am and this realisation blows my mind and scares me so much I start to shake. No one can tell me who I am. I am just a monster. That's all that people know me as. The police called me a monster. The judge called me a monster. Everyone I knew was frightened of me. Except for Etta. And the pain of that thought of Etta makes me sob and shake even more. I can't look myself in the eye, I say, because I'm scared of what the person behind the eyes has done. It's not me, that person. It's not me.

I agree, the counsellor says. I can help you know that person. It won't be easy but it is possible. And if you're prepared to work, to listen, to hear and to try to understand what passes through your mind, to focus and pay attention to your thoughts, then you have a future. It's you who will have to do the work.

I cry so much I start to gag. Then my breath catches, my heart is bouncing in my chest like a rubber ball. I'm addicted to my life. To my lifestyle. I don't know if I can be anything else because I don't know what anything else is like. I am scared to try. I'd never thought about the future past the next hit. Never even considered it, except to know that I'd die one day and I hoped I would be high and that it would be quick. I had no thought of giving up drugs. Hadn't imagined that it was possible to live without them. Everyone I'd ever met drank and took drugs.

I cough and reach for a cigarette and light it with shaking hands. I calm down as the little rush of nicotine tingles in my head and in my heart.

'OK,' I say. 'OK, I'll work.'

They helped me and helped with my rage but I couldn't get my head around many of the things they told me about addiction. Eventually I told them that I'd made a decision not to take drugs or drink alcohol.

When I see drink or drugs, I tell them, I will reject them. And I will keep doing that until it is part of who I am.

They try to talk me out of this plan. They think it is a bad plan; that I will fail. I tell them I won't and we go back and forth for a while. They say my chances of relapse are 99 per cent. Eventually we both agree we're just going to have to let me find out if I can survive in the outside as a sober person.

Alcohol is everywhere on the outside. There are two pubs in every street. Two off-licences, plus supermarkets with rows and rows of cheap booze. Everyone who lives in the halfway house drinks – high-strength, cheap beer and cider. The road outside reeks of it, from accumulated spillages and the smell of the men who stand, swaying, on the pavement, watching the world walk past. Alcohol isn't allowed in the house. Anyone caught drinking inside gets thrown out. I smoke a lot of cigarettes.

I work in a warehouse where they bake bread for a supermarket. It means getting up very early in the morning and so I sleep when most people are drinking. Sometimes I see the nightclub zombies staggering home or wherever on my way to work; they are out of their minds, their bodies doing their best to move on their own.

I do a lot of lifting and packing. The work is dull, repetitive and bad for my back, but I stick with it. In between, I think about killing myself and using drugs. If I use drugs then I will take up the life of an addict again. I will go to prison or die. I don't know what it is that is inside me that stops me from taking drugs or killing myself; I can think of no good reason not to do either of those things. Maybe it's because I feel as though I've been cheated out of something and if I stick around then maybe I'll get what it is I want.

This is where I meet Nadia. She's from Poland and I like her straight away. I didn't talk to her until she spoke to me. People tend to look at me and not talk to me much. I look like Bad News. When I look at myself in the mirror I see the shiny pink scars, the skin so thin and stretched on my knuckles and elbows that comes away if I twist too quickly while resting against something. The scar on my head is a good one, a thick pink line that would one day be white. My eyes are hooded and the skin around them is grey and swollen. I am twenty-five but I look so much older.

Nadia is beautiful – her eyes, skin, hair and figure – and I stare too much. I know it but I can't stop myself. At the same time, I don't how to talk to girls. I think of Etta and how we started talking and I can't remember. We were high and it just happened.

Nadia asks me my name and I tell her. She asks me where I'm from, what I did before and some other questions. I answer so that my past stays secret and then she says: 'Don't you want to ask me something?'

My mind goes blank.

Nadia speaks again: 'It helps to pass the time if you talk, you know?'

My mind is still blank.

After another moment, Nadia shrugs and turns around to a line of boxes and starts sticking labels on them. 'Suit yourself.'

I feel even more confused and then, suddenly, without knowing what I am going to say, I start to speak. I ask her where she's from and she tells me. I ask her how long she has been working here and she tells me. Once I get going I ask lots of questions, they just keep coming, about her family, what she likes, what music, where she goes to have fun, about work, her flat. I start feeling funny. The feeling is not exactly better than drugs but it is more whole, more complete, less of a rush and more of a high. Whenever I see her at the beginning of each shift it's like a hit. There's a sudden jump and then the feeling eases and holds. It doesn't fade. At some point I realise that I've fallen in love with Nadia and I don't know what to do.

Nadia has a boyfriend. A boyfriend. I did not do anything for several months except speak to Nadia. I wanted to be with her but I was scared, so scared. And now she has a boyfriend. He works in the bakery and he is a nice guy and I hate him and I want him gone. I see him talking to Nadia one day and then he talks about me. I look at Nadia too much, he says, and he calls me a weirdo. I feel rage and I know I have to walk away. I walk out of the building quickly. I'm shaking and sweating. The rage is so strong, I need an outlet. I am in an alleyway at the back of the factory and I see a wooden pallet leaning against the wall and I destroy it, with my fists, arms and feet. And it is in bits and I am still shaking and I don't feel any pain despite the blood on my hands. I keep walking, walking, walking, breathing hard. I smoke and breathe it in as hard as I can. I am an addict. The life of the addict is the same shit every day. There is no fun. No Good Times. There is no future. All I have is an obsession that overwhelms my body and mind. I am an addict to violence, an addict to drugs. I want both.

I stop at a greasy spoon and have a coffee and sit outside and smoke two cigarettes.

I go into the toilet and clean my hands and splash cold water on my face. I look into my eyes.

I want love. But no one sells love in a packet, pill or tube. I might never find love. But I want it and to know of it is enough to make me want to live.

Maybe one day.

I have another coffee, smoke two more cigarettes and then I go back to work.

Part Three:

THE OTHER SIDE OF LOVE

HOPE

Watching the files burn in our back garden with Dan. Kids in bed. Safe, warm, secure. I watch the flames swallow the past, the reports that said one thing, when something different had happened, that said things no one had ever told me. Many had cared and many had tried. But everyone has their limitations. It could have been better but it could have been worse.

I watch the fragments go up, carried by the heat.

Hope and her brothers . . . felt unable to cope any longer and took themselves off to the police station . . .

Wards of court . . .

The parents' . . . impossible behaviour . . . serious drink problems . . .

Hope is likely to be living at Chesterfields until she is eighteen.

As secure and supportive surroundings as possible . . .

No likelihood of the children returning home to live with their parents . . .

Hope being reported for criminal damage . . . close to her brothers . . . would like to go to a family with 'little kids in it'.

They thought they would be fostered . . .

They have a 'pie-in-the-sky' idea about fostering . . .

. . . terminating parental access . . .

. . . decided not to make a request to fostering and adoption . . .

. . . psychotherapeutic help . . .

. . . high-risk . . .

Hope has not had the childhood she should have had and she was . . . badly let down by her own parents . . .

We have not been able to make up for what Hope's parents have failed to do . . .

Until she can see that, if nothing else, professional people know their limitations and can face the pain this stirs up, there can be little hope that she will feel that she can truly trust anybody . . .

Holding out hope . . .

Now I knew. Even more so, now I knew and understood. Finally, for the first time in my life, I knew who I was – and I knew why.

Now I knew who I was, I needed to change some things.

I resigned from the Citizens Advice Bureau. The old me had become target-driven. I'd been driven by money and career progression. While I'd loved much of what I'd done and enjoyed earning money to pay the bills, I needed a new start. These were the people I'd worked and got drunk with. Just being there felt like the old me and I didn't like that person. It wasn't me anymore.

On the day I left, I called Danny.

'So,' he said, 'how does it feel?'

'Like, oh – my – God amazing,' I answered.

A new start – but as what? I'd left my job with nothing to replace it. The answer came, as so many things do these days, via Facebook. A message popped up from Carol, someone I knew through work. Carol was thinking of opening a night shelter for the homeless and I messaged her and we got talking.

She asked me what I was up to.

'I've just given notice.'

'Do you want a job?'

'All right then.'

It was that simple. I had to take quite a pay cut. I'd be paid less than half of my normal salary, which made things a bit hairy, financially speaking.

We persuaded six of our local Kent churches to fund us. We had just enough resources to provide shelter for four nights a week, for the four coldest months of the year. We 'advertised' via the police, who often dealt with long- and short-term homeless, and they promised to make sure that anyone who needed shelter knew what we were up to.

The plan was, starting every Friday night at 8pm and ending Tuesday morning, we'd go to one of the churches and convert it into a sleeping area, bringing hot dinners and breakfasts, as well as donated clothes and anything else we thought might be useful.

Come the first day, we were really nervous. It was a ridiculously small project and it was all volunteer-led. The local council didn't think there was a homeless problem but, of course, if you're not looking, you won't see it. We wondered whether anyone would actually come.

A trickle became a bit of a flood, as two dozen people arrived in quick succession and eventually we had over thirty cold and hungry people to deal with. The night flew past as we cooked, sorted clothes and spoke to everyone who came in.

People like me. People who had been abused and neglected, then lost and forgotten. I was already able to appreciate how lucky I was to have been in care until I was eighteen – not to have fallen through the cracks.

The next morning we cooked them breakfast. We buttered toast, fried eggs and bacon. When I said, 'Come and get it!' no one moved. 'What's wrong?'

One red-headed man in his thirties held up a shaking hand.

Without their morning hit of alcohol, they couldn't hold their cup of coffee, let alone eat and keep down breakfast. Carol and I cradled their coffees as they couldn't get the hot liquid anywhere near their mouths. The best we could do was give them a packed lunch and hand the building back to the church before lunchtime.

The police appreciated us keeping these people off the streets. It gave them more time to do other things. They'd call up and say something like, 'We've just seen Bill [a long-term homeless man] by the town clock but he's impossible. We can't control him at all. Bites, kicks, the lot.'

I'd go along with Carol and greet Bill with a cheery hello and a promise of a hot meal and a dry bed for the night and he'd come with us, quiet as a lamb. The police couldn't believe it. But it's simple, really. People like me, like Bill, like most people in this book, who've suffered abuse and neglect, can't handle people in positions of power and authority. I've learned to recognise this and my urges to run away, shout abuse or fight have been reduced to nothing, while poor old Bill sees in the police the countless people who've beaten him up and abused him since he was a child.

He was so unwell. Not only did we get Bill to come and see us, we talked him into going into detox after a few cups of tea.

We got thirty-two homeless people through one of the coldest, snowiest winters on record.

It felt amazing.

Then we managed to get more than a dozen long-term homeless people housed. People who'd been on the streets for a few days or weeks tended to be easier to deal with and were more motivated to sort out a permanent address than the long-termers, those who had forgotten what it was like to have a home.

I went to check up on one recently re-housed man and found a volunteer was already there, looking sheepish.

'What are you doing here?' I asked before realising.

They were together.

'I never expected to play Cilla Black when I started to work here,' I said. They are still together today!

Like many people who have suffered abuse and/or neglect, I wanted to do something to help people like me. I had my work with the homeless charity but I wanted to do more. I wanted to get closer to the people who found themselves in the position I found myself in as a child – as a ward of the state.

My chance came when a friend told me about an

opening at an independent fostering agency and I decided to go for it. I was plagued with fears about my ability – sometimes I was still overtaken by feelings that I was a fraud and was worried that I'd be caught out and exposed as a useless kid from care, who didn't deserve a place in society, who wasn't fit to be employed or respected as a professional. But, thanks to the love I received from the people who cared about me, I shoved these feelings aside and went for it.

There is something to be said for care leavers working in care. We've been through it and, if we're in a position to apply, then we're mentally robust enough to survive the job. We've done a lot of work on ourselves and our strengths and weaknesses. I get goosebumps when I meet people in the care system or care leavers who say they want to do outreach work or foster care. Kids in care really listen to adults who've been in care. They can be a valuable mentor because they can really say: 'I was in your position.' They can identify and deal with the tough questions kids ask. One young care leaver turned carer, a young man, had lived a wild life and a child he was caring for asked him if he'd had fun at the time.

'Yes, I did,' he replied. 'But I also went to a lot of funerals and I'm still visiting my old friends in prison.'

Getting the job at the independent fostering agency really was the culmination of all my hard work – finally to have the opportunity to use my own past to help others in the same position.

I really have come so far now. I have faced up to and dealt with my past. And I can accept the person I've become as a result. Not every day is perfect, of course, there are those lonely, grey days but that's something we all have to face in life. Now I have the mechanisms in place to cope.

I know that I am and have been loved – even when I sank into alcoholism. People believed in me and loved me enough to get me through the darkness and into the light.

I know from my own experiences that love is so important for children in care. My children are so affectionate with each other. We tell each other that we love each other every single day. Yet my parents didn't ever cuddle me and, as far as I could tell, they abhorred physical contact, even with each other. So where did my affection come from? From the people who showed me love in care, showed me that love was possible, that it was possible to give and receive love, and that love has the power to heal anyone.

LARS

I'm from a Scandinavian country and was trained there. It's quite different from the UK. Students of social work have to work in a children's home for at least three days each week. Just one day per week is spent at university. It takes four years to qualify. There's a lot of reading and group work, most of which is reflective – analysing your own thoughts, behaviours and emotions that emerge as responses to what's going on around you. This means that you have to spend a lot of time during those four years getting to know yourself extremely well. Of course, this is all supervised by a working social worker who assesses and guides you. It's an extremely interesting and rewarding experience. You learn how to build up trust with someone, so that you can give something of your true self to making the relationship work.

In the UK, I've sometimes observed how social workers are told not to talk about their own experiences, which I think is silly. It's good to make yourself vulnerable and this is critical in forging genuine relationships with children. In essence, we have to train the head, heart and hand (in terms of practical experience) to become a social worker. Too many people in the UK working in this sector are not confident in themselves. Everyone has their insecurities but maybe some social workers have insecurities that lead them to an attack-style – which leads the people we're trying to help to attack back, most often with allegations of unfair treatment or abuse.

Reflective study made it clear to me where my insecurities lay – removing them from their natural unconscious state to somewhere I'm fully aware of them. This doesn't happen in the UK and I think it needs to.

That is why, in the UK, there are guidelines for social workers and care home workers who want to hug the children they're looking after. Or perhaps I should say – not hugging them. I'm referring to the 'side hug', a sideways reach-around over the shoulder with one arm, designed to avoid inappropriate body-to-body contact.

There are so many things that are wrong with this type of advice, I barely know where to begin. When I give advice to my social workers, I am conscious of their safety and say that we've got a certain style of working, ethos, value and belief, and the side hug is most definitely not part of it. You wouldn't do that to your dog – why do it to a child? Only to protect yourself from a system that's gone bonkers.

When I first arrived in the UK and found work (I was given a job within a week in south London, they were really desperate), I was allocated a mother who needed to go and see her kids who were in foster care. We were in London, they were on the south coast. So I said I'd drive her down. The kids had been taken into care because of her alcohol and drug addiction.

Just as I was about to head off, my manager told me, 'You've got to take someone else with you. You can't go on your own with the mother in the car. Those are our safeguard rules.'

I argued that it was ridiculous; I wasn't worried about allegations because I wasn't going to do anything for her to make allegations about. I said there was no way I wasn't going to take this woman down to see her kids.

'At least make sure she sits on the back seat,' my manager replied.

I took her on my own, sitting next to me. We had only met twice but had a good relationship and trusted one another. These safeguard rules are only there to cover our backs. If anything, these rules are likely to worsen the relationships with the parents and children we work with by putting up barriers. In Scandinavia it was all about putting the child first, we never had to worry about this.

I had quickly established a relationship with the mother, who had many significant social and emotional issues, by being open and direct. I was unguarded, but not reckless. I kept her informed and made phone calls, trying to reassure her that I would keep her involved in her child's care and that there would be no nasty surprises.

The trip was beautiful. Her boy was a huge football fan and his whole room was a shrine to Liverpool, all red and gold. I'd never seen anything like this before back home and we had a good laugh about it.

I also invited the mother to meetings at our office. A review officer gave me a hard time about her coming along with her family. It was all to do with the child's wellbeing, I argued, so they should be here. The plan was for the mother's family to take a holiday near where the kids were staying, so she could see them more easily for a few days. I had assumed that this was what everyone did but it was quickly made clear to me that this was not the case. I was also surprised when people at case conferences would look at me and say: 'This is your case, you have to make a decision.'

Again, I felt as though this was all about them covering their backs, so I'd say something like, 'No, I don't think so. We all need to make a decision here. I'd like to discuss with you and then *we* can decide how *we* want to go forward with this case.'

This job is all about listening to people without making assumptions, wanting them to be part of the process.

The care home I worked in when I first arrived in the UK was a wealthy residential institution that cared for children aged five to seventeen. I had to supervise their showering and cleaning at the end of the swimming session, which would be full of rough-and-tumble sort of play. The care home had it set up so that was entirely normal. There was no policy. We just had to be there to make sure no one got hurt.

I read children bedtime stories, sitting on the side of the bed – girls and boys. If he or she wants to give me a hug then that's what they should get. After all the research into attachment theory, I can't believe we're denying warmth to the children who need it most.

All this is leading me to the story of Julius. Julius was a thirteen-year-old refugee from the Democratic Republic of the Congo and he arrived in the UK as an unaccompanied asylum seeker. He was placed with one of our foster carers. He spoke English but it wasn't that great.

I saw him a few weeks after dropping him off with the foster carers. I asked him how the placement was.

'Good.'

'So what's good about it?'

Julius looked down at his feet. He wouldn't say. I gave him time. This was a boy who'd seen his parents killed in front of him. He'd sustained serious injuries, been left for dead with deep stab wounds in his neck and chest. He was terribly traumatised.

I asked again, 'What was so good about it?'

He thought for a moment longer, then looked up: 'She gave me a hug.'

And I remembered it. The carer had opened the door, given him a great big hug and said, 'Come on in.'

I thought this was wonderful. I don't think anyone had touched him, except to take his fingerprints, since his parents had been murdered. This foster carer, with one simple act, had given the boy the one thing he wanted more than anything else – a simple act of love. The foster carer had shown him he *could* be loved.

If humanity is missing you're up against it; it's a massive thing to have missing from your life. That's often at the root of what we see in kids who've been neglected. Why would we want to carry on that neglect in our profession when it should all be about protection and healing? That applies to both children and their parents. I'm a normal human being and I get angry with parents who have neglected their children but, at the same time, I can still provide them with a level of respect, dignity and decency. Too many social workers are forced into box-ticking exercises with the people they're trying to help – completing forms with fifty questions when time spent on a more human approach would be far more valuable and would probably lead to a smaller chance of mistakes being made.

Science supports the idea that sensory stimulation by mothers (and fathers), i.e. touch, has long-term benefits in terms of its effect on a child's brain development. Animal experiments have taught us that babies who are never picked up die from stress. Babies who are born prematurely and are placed in incubators will have more rapid brain growth if they are touched for just a few minutes each day. Cuddling, holding and stroking all come naturally to humans. It reduces anxiety by creating more brain receptors for the naturally occurring tranquillising group of chemicals called benzodiazepines. When someone is addicted to tranquillisers, it says something about their childhood.

Children in foster care, most of whom are hoping for adoption, need all the cuddles they can get. Human beings need humanity. This shouldn't be an issue. It should be part of normality. We need to make a conscious effort to get away from worrying about covering our backs, from safeguarding rules, from the dreaded side hug.

Today, I tell my staff off for giving side hugs. I tell them about the movie *Good Will Hunting* with Robin Williams playing therapist Dr Sean Maguire and Matt Damon as Will Hunting, the troubled young man trying to re-evaluate his life and stay out of prison. At the end, Dr Maguire keeps saying to Will: 'It's not your fault.'

'What are you talking about?'

'It's not your fault.'

Will starts to break down and cry as he comes to accept that so much of what he's suffered and still is suffering is a result of the abuse he received as a child. Then, as the last bit of therapeutic input, Dr Maguire gives Will a really good, solid hug – something that had, up until then, been missing from his life. This leads Will to say: 'Does this violate the doctor-patient relationship?' and Dr Maguire replies: 'Not unless you grab my ass.'

HENRY

The flat was in a fairly pleasant estate in north London. I like to think I'm a fearless social worker but a feeling of dread crept over me as I started to ascend the four floors to the flat occupied by Gary and Nikki, both in their late twenties, and their two little boys, Anthony and Thomas – Tony and Tommy – five and seven years old.

I hadn't been in the job long and had just moved into the Looked After Children Team when the police called. I was first to pick up the phone, so that meant the case was mine. They needed me down at 'the scene' as they called it, as soon as possible.

The stink of urine, which I thought had been caused by some idiot peeing in the stairwell, got stronger and sharper, until I realised the smell was actually coming from the flat. Two small mongrel dogs had the run of the place and, it seemed, treated it like a toilet. The parents hadn't thought to clean up after them – or take them for a walk. But Gary and Nikki weren't the walking kind, which made me wonder why they had the dogs. Gary was even too lazy to walk upstairs to use the loo and he urinated in the kitchen sink, which was full of washing up. With the plug partially blocked, the fluids drained away slowly, soaking, then drying and sticking to everything, leaving an eye-watering, rank smell behind.

I'd never experienced anything like it before and I think even the police officers, who had been called in by the building manager, had been caught by surprise. How could anyone live in this mess? The kitchen was unusable, the floor sticky and covered in food. The lounge was full of newspapers, fast-food containers of every description, many with decomposing food and congealing sauces still inside.

A space had been cleared on the single worn sofa's dark green and shiny cushions, where Gary and Nikki sat and watched the large TV hanging on the wall at the other end of the room. The TV was the cleanest thing in the house by some margin.

The boys were perfect. Beautiful, fair-haired, and they looked well-fed and happy. They were scared of all these serious-faced strangers and clung to their parents. If you'd taken a snapshot of them together, you would have thought that this was a normal, loving family. And in many ways they were – save for the unbelievable mess.

I didn't want to touch anything but I slipped on a small car concealed under a discarded sock as I climbed the stairs and I had to grab the sticky banister to save myself from a backwards tumble.

The boys shared a room and it was cleaner than the rest of the house, although I found another small, scraggly dog sleeping in the lower bunk bed. It wagged its tail and grabbed a pillow in its jaws when it saw me, ready to play a game of tug-of-war.

There was a chest of drawers but, after I'd picked my way across the floor that was strewn with clothes and the occasional plastic toy, it almost came apart in my hands when I tried to pull open one of the drawers. It turned out to be empty.

I wondered about school uniforms. I eventually found trousers and shirts crumpled in the bottom drawer. They smelled stale. Hadn't the teachers noticed? Once in a while a child's uniform may not be the cleanest, but I suspected that this was a problem of terrifying consistency.

Both the boys were taken into foster care. They didn't want to go, and Gary and Nikki were heartbroken. I'm quite tall and I felt like I was towering over them (there was nowhere to sit) as I explained why I was there and what decisions were being made. They were small and Nikki was tiny, as quiet as a bird. When she did speak, Gary, who was nearer, would automatically repeat what she said so that I could hear. She wept silently when we took the two little boys in the police car to the foster carers, who lived a short drive away and had been warned about – and were prepared for – the head lice.

I worked with Gary and Nikki, trying to get them to improve their parenting skills, to deal with each other's emotional issues, and to clean up and keep the house in order. They'd listened and responded to everything I'd said positively but I didn't feel as though they really got it, or were committed to the process. I don't know if they thought I would eventually get fed up with them and with looking after their children and would just give them back but I got the sense they were simply biding their time.

Part of my job was to pay unannounced visits to see how they were getting on, and this is what scared me the most. I wanted Tony and Tommy to go home. I wanted them to have the parents that they loved so much back again. But I had to make sure my decision wasn't clouded by emotion. One of the many difficult things about this job is that I feel strongly for the parents and want them to have their children back so much that I have to force myself to be objective, to do what's right for the children. Sometimes doing the right thing means breaking the hearts of parents and children alike.

Also, this case was unusual. There was no indication that Gary and Nikki were deliberately abusing the children. It was just that they were failing to look after them on a spectacular scale. They had produced shining references from their employers (they delivered leaflets door to door, by the thousand, for a charity). Gary had a lot of medical problems and was in quite a bit of pain. It was easy to feel sorry for them. They didn't have much and worked hard for what they did have but, somehow, they couldn't see they were failing their children.

'All right, Gary. How are you doing?'

'Good, good thanks.'

'And Nikki?'

'Yeah, she's here. I'll put the kettle on.'

I was unlikely to drink it but said thanks anyway, hoping for the best.

'We've redone the house, as you can see.'

The house had indeed been redone, but by the council and by order.

I followed Gary, looking down on his near-black, thinning hair, for the nits. Yes, they were still there. We entered the lounge. Nikki, with her scraggly, fair hair, was shorter even than Gary. She got up from the sofa and whispered a greeting.

As they walked me through the maisonette, I saw they'd ripped out carpets and the walls and doors had been newly painted. But that sour urine smell was still most definitely there. Even though they'd gone along with the repairs (as long as they didn't have to bother to do anything themselves, they were fine), they hadn't changed their behaviour. Going along with things was a smokescreen to hide their inability to act. They weren't able to realise that we would see straight through this. That, in itself, was a little worrying. It wasn't a lack of intelligence, more a breakdown in thought processes, coupled with straightforward laziness and a remarkable ability to inhabit a pigsty. The strange thing was there was no trauma (that we were aware of) from either of their pasts that could have led to this. As far as we could tell, their childhoods hadn't been perfect but they hadn't been abused or neglected and had made it all the way through school. Both sets of their parents were very old and quite poorly and although they loved their grandchildren, they were in no position to take them in.

I'd dreaded going in but now, smelling the urine and seeing the mess in the kitchen, the food cartons in the lounge, a big puddle of what I guessed to be dried milk in the hallway, I started to feel relief. I would be certain in my decision. All I had to do was imagine Tommy and Tony coming back in here to live. It would be cruel.

Gary and Nikki weren't able to be honest.

'Still got the head lice?' I asked.

'Yeah, well, we tried that treatment but I don't think it was strong enough.'

Nikki whispered something.

'Nikki says we'll give it another go,' Gary added, sighing with annoyance. 'Wish they'd give us some stuff that actually worked.'

Most of the treatment for head lice involves wet combing with a fine-tooth comb and a lot of patience.

'It's not as if they do any harm, anyway. Not that serious, is it, lice?' Gary continued.

I wasn't going to confront them at this moment. One's approach is so important. Whatever happens, I'm going to have to deal with these people for several months. I need to be able to look them in the eye, to pay them a compliment when it's due, to be honest (unless it's in the child's interests, to get them out of danger) and to show them respect. Even the lousiest parent is human; they recognise respect, or the lack of it, and that can be key. Respect is a tricky thing because there's a fine balance between respect and pussyfooting, especially if a parent is abusing their children. There's been a lot of talk about social workers protecting their backs. I can't speak for others but I never thought about protecting my back. I talked honestly, and face to face. I've noticed that some social workers make themselves seem as though they're important, which makes others feel inadequate and leads to animosity. I feel most at ease when things are harmonious. There's a time for conflict, of course – after all, I'm here to do a job and work in the interest of the child, otherwise I'm not doing my job properly.

Therapists had worked with the boys and with the school to try and see if there was any way Gary and Nikki could meet their kids' long-term interests. While Gary and Nikki clearly loved their children, it was obvious that they were worlds away from being able to meet Tommy's and Tony's physical needs, let alone their practical and educational needs. And even though they loved their children, their emotional expressions were at best confusing for the boys.

It was clear cut.

The boys wanted to go home and the parents wanted them to go back.

But I couldn't see any reason for these children to go home. They would have a much better chance in care. Things had not improved enough, in my opinion. We always try to work towards significant improvement but if we feel the parents could fall back into neglectful behaviour at any moment, then it's better for the children not to be put through the experience again – as well as another separation.

Tommy, the oldest, was most affected by the lack of parental care. His self-esteem and self-worth was non-existent. I didn't think there was any chance that the parents could have made up for what went before. If they had kept a clean house, provided their children with breakfast and walked them to school and back, then I would have thought there was a chance, but it was clear that these parents weren't ever going to be able to provide even this. Tony would soon be suffering from the same disordered psychological symptoms as Tommy.

It was possible that Gary and Nikki could have kept them alive, i.e. fed and watered the boys until they were able to leave home. Or they could be cared for by other people who would work on their emotional wellbeing as well as their general care. The therapeutic aspect of a child's life is so important. Of course, we have to make sure we've done everything we can to assess and support families in a safe way but there's only so much you can do.

It's an awful decision to have to make, especially when parent and child love each other, but they would have a much better chance in care. Tommy and Tony really wanted to be with their mum and dad. I don't think they understood at all why they had to go. Walking out of that block with those little boys was so hard but at the same time, this was what it was all about. Saving kids before the damage was done, placing them in a caring, loving environment that would allow them to grow and become the wonderful grown-ups they deserved to be.

Although I'd made it clear that I had grave concerns for the parent's capacity to care, and even though the council sided with me at court, the judge decided that Tommy and Tony, rather than go into long-term fostering and then adoption, would go back to their parents, albeit with a care plan and community monitoring in place.

I felt really strongly against this. I couldn't understand the judge's decision. This is risk management, deciding which side you're prepared to err on. But the child shouldn't ever have the risk, nor the trauma of coming in and out of their parents' lives. Tony and Tommy had, by this time, been in foster care for six months, which, for them especially, was a huge amount of time.

As far as I was concerned, the judge had put the parents' needs before the children's needs.

Sometimes bad decisions get made when the parents find really good solicitors and barristers who make a really good case, especially when the local authorities find themselves caught on the back foot thanks to people leaving the job and the case being passed on to new, inexperienced workers who are unfamiliar with the family. They also don't have as much time to spend on case preparation. Due to case workloads, transfers, illness, pregnancy and retirements, a family's social worker might change several times, while the family's solicitor stays the same all the way through.

Judges may want to come down on the side of social services but if the evidence isn't presented well enough, then they don't have that option. Judges also tend to think that parents should be given another chance. It's understandable that they don't want to be the monster that makes the final decision that will break up the family.

In the case of Tony and Tommy I wrote letters to the director of social services with my opinion: 'I want this to be recorded, on my file and on the children's file: I fundamentally and entirely disagree with the plan.'

They arranged a phone conference. The director went through the case, point-by-point.

'A lot of what you say, we agree with. It's not what we asked the court for but the court decided something else, so this is the plan.'

'I'm nervous about it.'

'So are we. We will be subject to a serious case review, not the judge, if something happens to the children.'

Perhaps the worst part for me was visiting the foster carers to give them the news. Robert and Anna were in their thirties and lived in a lovely little house on the corner of a quiet street almost next door to an enormous and idyllic park with two children's play areas. They couldn't have children of their own and, rather than opting for IVF, had decided to care for children in need.

'We just didn't like the idea of IVF,' Robert, who ran his own small building company, told me. 'When we first considered the idea, the doctor sent us to the hospital along with dozens of other couples for a lecture all about the process and something didn't feel right. It's not as straightforward as most people think. There are risks. Anna just came out with the idea when we were driving home and it felt right. So here we are.'

This was their first long-term foster placement and, despite their lack of experience, they had done an amazing job. Their house was, as one would expect, clean, warm and cosy. They'd made a photo album of all the adventures they'd had with Tommy and Tony and it was clear to me that the boys had come to love their foster parents and their life in this new home.

Robert and Anna were devastated when I told them Tommy and Tony would be going home to their parents and were just as surprised and hurt by the decision as I was.

At the moment, foster carers don't have the status where they are able to be part of the process at all. They're not even consulted, because they don't have any degree or qualification; they're not seen as professionals. But they are professional and, most importantly, they're part of the family. Foster carers have to jump when social services or the court dictates without pre-consultation. They have to do what they're told – to be impossibly flexible and shock resistant – in that they can lose the kids they've been looking after for months within a very short space of time.

'We love the boys so much,' Robert said. 'We'd do anything for them. Now they go back, and the undoing of everything we've tried to do will begin. After all the work we've done, this is the result?'

I couldn't argue with them. The love Robert and Anna had for Tommy and Tony, which had grown into a love as strong as any parent, had led to massive positive change in the boys' quality of life.

Gary and Nikki's feelings of love, poorly expressed to me but cleverly explained in the courtroom by a talented solicitor, had been enough to convince the judge, though. I'm convinced that if Robert and Anna had had a voice then the outcome would have been all the better for Tommy and Tony. It wasn't long before I observed that Gary and Nikki had failed to fulfil basic hygiene needs once again, let alone provide their kids with stimulation – they just couldn't be bothered. They loved their kids but had very little will to care for them. Gary and Nikki showed me that love on its own isn't enough, that love alone doesn't provide children with everything they need.

ISABEL AND ANDY

It had taken a month of treatment to wean Patti off the opiates. Then she spent eighteen months in foster care. And now we had her. Suddenly, we had a child.

I'd hoped I'd love her from the first moment and I did.

When I held Patti for the first time I took in her smell, her hair, the miniature nails on tiny pink toes, each one as perfect as its neighbour, her eyes full of wonder and the soft little sounds that came from her perfect mouth. I was smitten. For almost a year, I'd hoped and hoped this was how I would feel and now that I did, I was overjoyed.

Thinking about it now, it was a bit like falling in love with a new partner – an infatuation that's a bit different from the love between mother and child. Love comes with time. I was just too excited and happy to notice the difference right then.

The fear came later. It started to creep in after a couple of weeks, when life didn't return to 'normal', when the worry that some harm could come to Patti grew into outright fear – fear that I might harm her accidentally, through some negligent act that no other mother would be silly enough to make. Just as strong was the fear that something would happen that I would be unable to prevent, something that would be totally beyond my control.

I'd leave the house with Patti so swaddled she looked like the Michelin Man. For me, the outside world was a place full of hazards: slippery concrete staircases; reckless cyclists who would crash into the pushchair; joggers who would knock her from my arms; escaped lunatics who would snatch her away from me.

My heart would start pounding as I neared the park on our daily outing. What about dogs? How would I stop a dog from attacking her? I zigzagged my way across the park, cutting back and forth, avoiding dogs and the unsavoury-looking types who seemed to be everywhere these days.

With the fear came doubt. Thoughts that I couldn't do this. That when I had sworn before a court, in front of a judge, that I would do anything to keep this child safe under my protection, I had lied.

Patti was difficult to feed and often irritable, wailing unexpectedly, when something wasn't just right. Her cry terrified me, especially at night. It was so sad, like she was mourning, as if she was in pain or lamenting – maybe for her real mother.

I would go to her with Andy but she carried on wailing no matter what we did, until she was exhausted and sleep claimed her once more. She also wailed whenever I put her down during the day, leading me to pick her up and hold her for hours at a time. I just couldn't bring myself to leave her in her pram or cot for any length of time. Every time she wailed I felt like I was failing. I had to stop it.

I'd been warned that some of this behaviour came as a consequence of the heroin her mother took; but I wasn't helping. If anything, I was reinforcing her behaviour and, although I knew this, I didn't know how to stop myself, to change what I was doing. I was inexperienced and didn't have the answers.

Maybe I didn't deserve to be a mother. This was a fear that came from the fact that I couldn't have children. Neither of us could. My husband had a low sperm count and the sperm that were there were, in the words of the report, 'sluggish'.

When I mentioned this theory of mine to Andy, he dismissed it but I knew he felt it, too. We had spent a long and unpleasant period grieving for the fact that we were unable to have children. We'd tried for two years before admitting defeat and going to the doctor. And then we each went through the humiliation of testing and 'failing'. The next possible option was IVF, for which we turned out to be poor candidates; there was no point in us trying.

Each stage had been a blow – not being able to conceive naturally, then finding out there was something wrong with us, then being rejected even for IVF, which everyone seems to think is so easy these days.

So we decided to adopt. We both loved the idea of giving a child in desperate need a home. It was a stressful process, a strange thing to go through as an adult. You have to place your life, your history and your family and even your friends under great scrutiny – and open up like never before to complete strangers. No matter how good the social workers are, it all feels a bit one-sided, and you spend months feeling as though you're being judged.

The whole road to Patti was a series of stressful events.

Now we had her, all that stress was coming out.

In the UK four babies are born every day addicted to heroin, crack or other drugs. That's around 1,500 babies every year, all of them entering the world suffering from 'neonatal withdrawal symptoms'. Not the greatest of introductions to the world. I couldn't believe that Patti had been one of them. She was so perfect and such a delight – but she kept falling ill. She came down with several bugs, then an eye infection, followed by a stomach infection that gave her a fever which terrified me beyond words.

Patti's mother hadn't wanted to meet us. Social services said there would have been complications attached to any meeting anyway, as she had become closely associated with some serious criminals.

Still, I would have liked to meet her. Maybe it would have helped me to know what kind of woman kept taking heroin while she was pregnant. It might also have helped me to make the mother realise that this outcome was the best option and that she could at least know we were going to take good care of Patti.

Perhaps I was hoping she would give me a reason not to feel anything bad towards her – that she had been a victim of circumstance and couldn't keep her baby, as much as she might have wanted to. Instead, I wondered whether the part of the mother that made her go off the rails was in

Patti. Was the same fate waiting for her, years down the road? I'd heard stories of adopted children falling apart when they reached their teens.

I still wasn't sure what to tell Patti about her birth mother. This thought weighed heavily on my mind, as did the fact that Patti was not my child. I was not her mother. I was a substitute. Maybe that meant I could never be her mother, our bond could never be *that* close.

I was supposed to be the winner in this situation. I had the baby I'd so desperately wanted. But I didn't feel like that at all. Andy moved the cot into our room and I lay awake listening to Patti sleeping at night, checking every few minutes when I couldn't hear her breathing, looking to see her chest rise, make sure that her face was uncovered.

Every day my doubts grew. I was helpless. Cot death, dogs, accidents, viruses and diseases. I couldn't fulfil my promise. I couldn't keep Patti safe from all those things. I wasn't her mother. She wouldn't love me. She would grow up to be a drug addict.

I barely ate and only showered when Andy told me I should; I didn't bother to change and let my clothes pile up, then I stopped changing. I was on alert throughout the night and resented Andy's casual and uncaring ability (as I saw it) to sleep right through. When he tried to talk to me about how I was feeling, I'd get angry. He didn't understand. He was a man. He couldn't possibly understand what I was going through. I wasn't a mother; I didn't know what to do – how 'real' mothers did it.

After the stress of the night came the lonely day filled with fear. I worked from home and hadn't taken maternity leave. After all, I hadn't actually been pregnant and given birth, had I? I just brought a fully formed little girl home and was ready to go. My friends had left me alone, telling me I must be rushed off my feet with friends and family wanting to see the 'new arrival'.

I cried for no reason. Went to bed exhausted. Woke up after what felt like five minutes' sleep that came the moment the room started to lighten – I'd made it through another night. But now my heart filled with dread as the day lay before me – night-time was, if anything, the safest; hours of precious isolation in the bedroom.

This was all so crazy because Patti was wonderful. She gave me no cause to doubt her. She giggled, played and was full of desire to learn everything about this amazing, magical world she found herself in.

Eventually, I would go to bed wishing I wouldn't wake up the next morning.

The doorbell rang. This was Lisa, our social worker, who'd seen us through the adoption and was now coming by to check up on us as we moved towards the day when Patti would be decreed ours by the courts, when we would have just the same rights as any parent in relation to their child.

I dreaded it with every fibre of my being. I tried to stop shaking as I looked at my trembling fingers, smoothed down my clothes, plastered some kind of smile on my face and opened the door.

Lisa was about the same age as me, mid-thirties. I didn't know that much about her personally, but she'd been kind, professional and genuinely interested in how Andy and I were doing throughout the adoption process, as we crossed off each milestone on our way to our dream of having our own child.

And that was a problem. She knew us both well. I was terrified that she was going to see how badly I was failing, the bags under my eyes, my run-ragged look (I'd lost a lot of weight), the clothes shoved behind the sofa, the wash basket filled to the brim. That she would see Patti looking ill and letting rip with her mournful wail and then she would know I was failing to provide Patti with the environment I'd sworn to provide her with that day in court. And that would mean she would take Patti away. I was a total failure as a mother. I'd spent so long trying to adopt and now I was going to lose my baby through neglect, through my sheer incompetence.

I'd made a superhuman effort to clean up for Lisa. Teapot, mugs and the good biscuits were on the kitchen counter.

It only took her five minutes to notice.

'I think you have something called Post Adoption Depression,' she said. I genuinely didn't understand. My mind had a 'Say what?' moment.

'I know,' Lisa continued. 'You didn't go through pregnancy, the morning sickness, the physical and hormonal changes. You didn't face the excitement and fear of delivery and you're not breastfeeding. Your hormones aren't all over the shop, right?'

I nodded, still unable to speak, unable to keep the fear from my face.

'It's a fairly recent discovery. For years there's been anecdotal reports but, in the last few years, some serious scientific studies suggest that one in five adoptive mothers suffer from this.'

'But I'm not depressed,' I said. 'I've never had depression.'

But I'd suffered all the symptoms Lisa then listed: extreme fatigue, unrealistic expectations of parenthood; a lack of community support. Coupled with this are the assumptions people make about adoptive parents; the belief that the mother who doesn't go through pregnancy and childbirth doesn't need as much, if any, help, as a natural mother does.

'Did you take maternity leave?' Lisa asked.

I shook my head.

'Thought so. Classic sign. You didn't feel there was a need. You hadn't been in hospital and given birth. By not being pregnant and not giving birth you hadn't earned it. But that doesn't mean you couldn't do with some support from friends and family – some help around the home, to help clean up and – heaven forbid – babysit to give you some respite.'

Lisa smiled, looking at Patti who was clinging on to the sofa by Lisa's knees and slapping it with her hands, enjoying the feeling. 'Besides, I can tell that this little madam is a full-time job.'

Lisa suggested that I should talk to a qualified therapist and that, perhaps, if the therapist thought so, I should see my doctor to talk about the symptoms of depression. For some, mild antidepressants can help. She would check in with me every few days to see how I was doing.

I promised Lisa I would and, once she left, I realised she was trusting me to take care of Patti while I worked through this Post Adoption Depression.

I told Andy and we told each of our parents. Then I told a couple of trusted friends. Not only was it a great unburdening, the help I then received was so much better than I could have imagined. Having a little time away from Patti to readjust, day by day, to her presence and to start enjoying her development, the things that amused and amazed her. The fear and anxiety stayed for a long time but eventually started to fade. I slept for longer at night. But still I worried about the effect of Patti's past on her future and this dominated my thinking, it was almost all I thought about.

A few months later, I was walking in the park with Patti – who was now chasing unsteadily after dogs and squirrels, something I would have found intolerable not long ago. I crouched down with her to look at a fearless squirrel that was watching us, hopeful for food, just a few feet away. As I did this, for the first time I noticed the squirrel, I mean really saw it, and suddenly I was present in the moment with Patti – being fascinated by the funny, furry, cartoon-like creature sitting on its haunches watching us closely. It was the first time I'd been able to be truly present, not obsessed by my usual gamut of worst fears: that I would somehow let my baby come to harm, that I wouldn't be able to adjust to this new presence in our lives, or be able to live with the fact that there was this other world from which Patti came, that she would grow up and hate me, that I would lose her, that I could never be her mother. Suddenly I was enjoying the moment – I was in the here and now. At that moment, as if to reward me, Patti threw her arms open wide and launched herself, lips first, against my cheek. My first true moment of happiness as a mother.

And I started to appreciate every moment my baby had to give me – my depression had taught me to enjoy what I had right here in front of me. Take care of today – and tomorrow, with all its unknown dangers, will take care of itself.

SEAN AND CARL

We'd come a long way for this moment – mentally and physically, across space and time. Several months and several hundred miles from home. Now we were on the verge of achieving the dream of having our own son. But first, we were going to meet his mother in a nondescript room in a social services office about three hours' drive from our home. We were early, she was late. While we waited, we made nervous, awkward conversation with a social worker we hadn't met before.

We'd both wanted children for as long as I can remember. When we first put ourselves forward we faced a long wait and assessment before we were eventually approved to adopt two children up to the age of six. Most people tend to put in requests for children closer to baby age rather than school age, but it was still early days for gay couples in terms of adoption – like many of the older children out there waiting for adoption, we were at the bottom of the pile. This has since changed, as agencies have started to place more children with gay couples.

We were quite open – boy or girl, any age up to six was fine with us. It was more about a sense of personality and we hoped we could get a feel for that from the child's appearance, once we saw a photo. As much as social workers don't want them to, looks do play a part, especially when that's all you've got to go on in the first instance to find something to bond with.

We had researched the subject of adoption and it was quite frightening. We'd learned that it's not easy at all. Some adoptive parents had been left at their wits' end by children who – damaged by abuse, living out incredible anger, fear and pain – had kicked, hit and hated, day-after-day, and the parents who gave them so much love, got almost nothing back.

I didn't think I could manage that. I don't think I've got what it takes to be that resilient. We never expected adoption to be that challenging. I didn't think we could go as far as these other adopters who took on the most troubled children. I wondered if many of these adopters of older children had their eyes wide open. Saying, 'Oh, we're happy with children of any age,' is great, but they need to talk to other adopters of children that age, which is something our social worker encouraged. The teenage years will hit these children hard – not because of hormones as for most kids, but because that's when the childhood trauma comes back.

Because our local authority was struggling to find us a child of any age, we looked further afield. We were amazed to discover that there were agencies who supplied you with catalogues. Photos of dozens of children looking into the lens for their forever home – there seemed to be more boys than girls, and lots of brothers, no doubt desperate to stay together.

Another council a long way from home got in touch. 'I'm sorry we can't tell you much,' the caller said. 'But we have a twelve-month-old boy you might be interested in adopting. The reason I can't tell you much is that there are some serious issues with regard to some of the people the mother is associated with.'

'Can we see a photo?' I asked.

'No, not at this time, sorry.'

'What's his name?'

'I can't tell you right now, but if you're interested then we will come down to see you and tell you more.'

Well, there was nothing there for us to fall in love with but after a quick chat with Carl, it was clear to us both that our instincts were telling us to go for it.

So this baby boy's social workers travelled down from the Midlands to visit us. We were both so nervous. It felt like such a big deal. I'm used to tough interviews and presentations – I run my own business – but I was really nervous, as was Carl, who was used to dealing with all kinds of children in his job as a primary school teacher. After years of hard work and saving, we felt like we were finally in a position to raise a family and Carl was planning to take some time away from work to be a stay-at-home dad for a few years.

We talked with the social workers for an hour or so, mainly about ourselves. As things were drawing to a close, I asked if we could see a photo. They took out a file, unhooked a picture and we saw this little boy for the first time. He was beautiful.

'Can we know his name?'

'Donald.'

I looked at Carl and I could tell he was feeling just as emotional as I was. We still had so little to go on but we knew we wanted to keep going, whatever was waiting for us. We were both speechless for a few moments before we could finally say that we were ready.

We understood their caution with regard to information. If you're told too much right at the start, then it may be that you'll be scared off. And maybe no one will ever come forward. At the same time, there has to be a balance so that you aren't left with a misleading rosy picture. All we knew was that his birth mother, Michelle, as well as being associated with some unpleasant people, was a drug addict and had been unable to end her dependency on heroin. That's the way adoption has changed. Fifty years ago, most adopted children came from unwed mothers abandoned by the father of their child, left unable to support their children (or to find a husband to support them). These days it seems that they come from drug addicts.

MICHELLE – A YEAR EARLIER

The nurses had changed.

They thought I was asleep but I couldn't. I just lay, quietly, waiting until they would let me go, or would leave me alone, so I could go and score. I badly needed to score.

They'd been nice at first when the taxi had dropped me off. Arms around me, lots of questions: 'Is it your first?' 'Who's your doctor?' 'Who should we call?' 'Any medical conditions we should know about?'

I knew that my answers – Yes; don't have one; no one (except maybe my mate Del, who could bring me some drugs); and Yes, but I'm not telling you 'cos I know that will lead to trouble – would not go down well. So I just sighed and moaned and collapsed on to a trolley, where I lay until they found me a bed.

Things changed once they spotted the track marks on my arms, the scabs and scars, and the rash I'd got from scratching and picking at imaginary insects when I was high.

Now, excitement long over, lying in the dark in the small hours as the nurses rattled around with their trolley filled with pills, I overheard one of them say: 'If she loved her baby she would have stopped taking drugs.'

I didn't know I was pregnant for two months. And then Del said it was dangerous for the baby to stop taking heroin. Not that I needed much of a reason to keep going. Being pregnant, I could have leapt right into a methadone programme, but I didn't consider that. Methadone, heroin – one drug was as bad or as good as another, as far as I was concerned.

Now my baby was being fed methadone, an addict just like her mum.

He looked normal, beautiful. But the seizures weren't. They started a few hours after he was born, and were followed by fever. The nurses had already alerted the doctor, and when he came I could tell he knew. He didn't say anything and he was nice, but there was a look in his eyes that I recognised.

And now the baby was in a neonatal high-dependency unit. He. I didn't even have a name for him.

I was the evil mother whose baby was born addicted to heroin. Was I that person? I never hurt anyone. All my life I've been a victim. But I had to admit the facts: I was that junkie who took drugs all the way through her pregnancy.

My baby's better off without me. Better off here. With these nurses who hate me and love him.

They eventually left with their trolley on the midnight run. I sat up. I felt rough as hell but I was able to walk.

It's amazing what you can achieve when you're being driven by something even more powerful than love.

I was a drug addict. My addiction defined me. We're seen as liabilities; the root of all crime, and much of the country's social ills. People quickly give up on you once they know you're a drug addict. It's a natural response. We value our health and general wellbeing less than the possession and intake of drugs, drugs that eat away at our bodies, making us ill, killing us slowly. Even when we're seriously ill, we won't do anything to change that – or let anyone help us.

It's easy to judge. And I also think that it's impossible not to.

My mum was an alcoholic. When my dad left, Mum used the hall cupboard as a babysitter, locking me in – I was eighteen months old – while she went out drinking. Mum had another child after me, Colin, 'Col', who died aged seventeen from a drugs overdose.

I tried to come off drugs several times but failed every time. When I was seven weeks pregnant, I started going to a drop-in centre, where I frequently threatened to kill myself. At this time, I was using more heroin than I ever had. I wanted my baby and I wanted to stop using heroin. Both of these things turned out to be impossible.

People just know. It's like they can smell the drugs a mile off. They avoid me. They see me but they don't see me, like I'm invisible. Like stepping over the cracks in the pavement, they steer around me. Heaven forbid they should touch a junkie like me. I just don't feel right until I'm inside with my own kind and high.

To me 'normal people' live in a world that I don't understand and a world that rejects me wholeheartedly. I see it on TV. It's like nothing I know. I just live day-to-day.

In between the rages, the binges, I suffer awful moments of reality. The kind of reality that brings the kind of pain that only the drugs will stop. I know my addiction comes from my past and the emotional state it's left me in. Only illegal highs can numb my reality.

I've been told, time and again, variations of: 'Your actions bring about awful results, so stop them.'

If only it were that simple. I bet you do one of the many things that are bad for you: drink, smoke, eat fast food, stay up too late, watch too much TV, gamble, get into debt, pay for sex.

There are no pills that can stop my addictive desire.

And when you look at it objectively, you have to wonder why anyone would put something into their body that is a poison which is slowly killing them (or might kill them through overdose or some kind of contamination), that leaves them insensible, unable to function, to understand and interact with other human beings, to care for their child?

Drug addicts are more afraid of life than death. Death is easy, it comes naturally to the addict. Life, on the other hand, is full of pain. Why do we use words such as 'it hurts' when talking about emotions? Or say that something is painful to discuss? The pain centres in our brain are tied up with our emotional centres and opiates connect with both. Whatever the addiction, it is born of pain and feeding that addiction somehow combats the pain – but only temporarily of course. For the hours that the drugs blank out the pain, there is the awakening, the comedown, when everything feels worse, when the pain and emptiness return.

Drugs kill emotions along with feelings of emptiness; they eliminate boredom, loneliness, weariness; they make you feel like you're worth something and give you the confidence to deal with other people.

You have to ask addicts like me, not why we take drugs – I take drugs so that I don't feel like I do when I don't do drugs, so I don't feel the awful pain that is my life – you should ask us where the pain comes from.

Everyone suffers from painful emotions at some time in their lives; it's part of being human. We all cope in different ways and people who have been abused as children have a lot more pain to deal with than most. Nearly all of us addicts have suffered serious abuse as children, whether it was neglect, or physical, psychological or sexual abuse or a mixture of some or all of the above.

I saw my own addicted mother turn to prostitution to support herself, repeating what she saw her mother do. Don't forget that addicts like me were once the children we now feel so sorry for when we hear of terrible stories of abuse on the news. Learn to love and try to help all humans, not just the children.

I was three months pregnant when I trashed the kitchen at the drop-in centre. The microwave was on the floor, along with broken plates and the remains of a Pot Noodle. I was trying to pull the cupboard from the wall, and had almost succeeded, the door was hanging from one hinge, when I collapsed on the floor, sobbing.

What had set it off? I had seen my face in a small mirror hanging on the kitchen wall. I could see a young woman and an old woman at the same time, my face thinning and falling apart thanks to all the drugs I'd wasted my life chasing. I was in a giant hole, alone with my mind, the mind that wouldn't shut up and wanted to talk about my past – all the terrible things.

I didn't have enough money for my fix and I was in pain, physical, mental and emotional. It seemed as though my face could only express distrust, anguish, fear and helplessness. Drugs gave me a sense of what that childhood would have been like without pain.

I was sexually abused by my step-father for several years before I ran away from home aged seventeen. This was just a short time and yet a whole lifetime ago.

I was twenty-two years old.

Drugs take away the pain but they also add to the pain.

I wanted to keep my baby. I believed my baby would somehow make it all right. I never considered having an abortion. I wanted the baby more than anything. But to do this meant giving up the heroin. To demonstrate to my social workers that I was truly determined.

I nodded along with my social worker and fully agreed with her, believing with all of my heart that: 'No one was going to take my baby from me.'

My history was stacked heavily against me.

As it was too dangerous for my baby to withdraw from the opiates during pregnancy (there's a danger of neurological damage), it was better that the addiction was dealt with using methadone after the birth. I was supposed to attend a methadone programme.

The father, who was around for a while, had made vague promises to do the right thing and support his child, but he disappeared when I was six months pregnant. I was devastated. I was still using heroin and hadn't attempted to enter a methadone programme.

'You will lose your baby,' the social worker said. 'You can't be a good mother if you're having to buy heroin every day.'

'I'm stopping, I'm stopping, really I am.'

'You have to. Otherwise you'll lose your baby.'

I gave birth to a healthy (albeit opiate-addicted) little boy. It was a fairly straightforward process to deal with the opiate dependence. Less so for me when I heard my baby had been taken into emergency protection. I remember being so, so fucking angry, and I was hit by a rage the likes of which I'd never known.

I screamed over and over: 'He's my fucking baby! They won't let me see him! My fucking baby! He's mine, mine, he's all I have!'

Now I've lost my baby and that means more pain. For a while I deluded myself with fantasies of getting him back. But I couldn't stop the drugs.

For a while I had a therapist and he told me that people who have been abused have an understandable fear of authority and of anyone with power. I could identify with that. I had been victimised by the powerful once more, which only increased my sense of helplessness, before I was told that I wasn't fit to be a mother. The child needed to come first, be the number-one priority. Security and emotional stability are key. Impossible to provide when you're high.

I knew. I came to accept that my baby needed to be with someone who lived in that alien world most people call 'normality'. This would be the most selfless thing I could do as a mother.

But, of course, giving away your baby only adds to the pain.

Something else for the drugs to deal with.

SEAN AND CARL

As the day of the meeting drew near, we grew increasingly anxious. Karen, our social worker, did her best to put us at our ease.

'She's coming to meet you,' Karen told me over the phone. 'She's accepted the decision and now she's accepting you. This is a confirmation, a reassurance.'

'I'm so nervous. What if she doesn't like us?'

'You're nervous, she's nervous. More nervous than you. She believes she's the one at fault here, the woman who couldn't be a mother to her child, unlike millions of other women. She's going to worry about rejection a lot more than you. You have many more reasons, she thinks, to reject her. She needs you to like her.'

'I suppose. But what if we don't like her? Suppose we just don't get on.'

'Well that could happen, but I think it's unlikely. We're all here because we want what's best for Donald. Just be yourself. That's who she wants you to be.'

'What are we going to talk about?'

'She's going to want to know all about you. You might want to bring a photo album of you growing up, include your families. It gives you something to look over and it's a really good way for them to get a sense of who you are.'

'What can we ask her?'

'Best to avoid sensitive questions, about the father and so on. His history, the drug use, violence etcetera. We can answer those sorts of questions. Just be positive and let her know how delighted you are to become parents. At the same time, be sensitive to her thoughts about her own failure to become a capable mother.'

On the morning, I got up at dawn. I was really worried about what to wear. 'If you think twice about any item of clothing, then you probably shouldn't wear it,' Carl advised. The bed was soon covered in shirts, T-shirts and jumpers.

'At least you didn't try any ties,' Carl said. 'What would you have put on if this was Saturday morning and we were going into town? Just as long as it's clean and free of wrinkles.'

Pushing thoughts of the meeting to one side for a moment, I chose a plain jumper and jeans.

'So, shall we make a move?' I asked, as Carl nodded approval.

'We're not meeting until this afternoon; we've got hours before we need to leave yet.'

'What about traffic? Good parents would always be on time, wouldn't they?'

Carl gave me a look.

'I'm sorry,' I said. 'I'm just so nervous.'

'Me, too.' We hugged. This was such a big deal. I didn't realise quite how much I'd be affected by meeting the birth mother. Were we good enough to be parents?

The door opened and a social worker entered, smiling, with a young woman, pale, thin and below average height, dressed in skin-tight black jeans, black trainers and a white top with a denim jacket. She looked as scared as I felt. Somehow we made it through the introductions and sat down.

I'm well known for foot-in-mouth syndrome and this was really dangerous territory for me. The first thing I said was, 'Oh, Donald takes after you. I mean . . .'

Carl looked appalled.

She laughed and that broke the ice. From that moment on we discussed our family, what they all thought about us being gay – how we came out – and then about what they thought about us adopting children and whether we planned to adopt any more children, which we did. Luckily our families were very supportive of us both, and we had two pairs of grandparents we could rely on to help us.

And then she asked: 'How will you tell Donald about me?'

'From the start,' I said. 'We'll always let him know about his other family, his mum, so it's normal for him from the beginning. We don't want to keep secrets and it's kind of obvious, us being a gay couple, that we've adopted, anyway, so he'd realise from a very young age, even if we didn't tell him.'

Our plan was to have letterbox contact, a method by which Michelle could keep in touch with us, just to know that everything was OK and she could, as long as her social worker approved, write to Donald and even send him photographs and Christmas and birthday presents.

'So there is a place for me in Donald's life?'

'Well, yes, we certainly don't have a problem with that. I think we have to run everything by your social worker but that's fine with us, too.'

'I'm a heroin addict,' she said. 'But I'm going to stop.'

This led to a slightly longer pause before Carl said: 'I'm sure you will.'

Then Michelle said she had to go. It was obvious this had been much harder for her than it had been for us.

A few weeks later, shortly before Donald was due to arrive at his new home, we received a package from Michelle. It contained a framed photo of her and a neatly handwritten letter. Carl and I immediately sat down to read it together:

I wanted Donald more than anything in the world. I never considered abortion. He was a wanted baby and I need you to know that. I love him so much. I loved being pregnant with him and, thinking of that time, there are real moments of happiness for me.

I put my own needs first and that was wrong. But by accepting you both as his parents, I hope I have done the best thing I could for my son, and that one decision will make his life as good as it can be, whether I am there or not. It is a decision I came to accept as his mother and I hope Donald will know that I only made this decision because I wanted to be a good mother but I just couldn't at this time in my life. More than anything I want to be able to look Donald in the eye and tell him how much I love him, and to hold him, hug him, like he needs to be hugged. I know I have to make some changes if this is to happen. I also hope that you will tell him about me and pass on my messages to him whenever you can and will help me make sure that he understands why this had to happen. I wish I could be there to explain to him in person but, as long as he knows I love him, care for him and want to be a part of his life, then I can go forward with my life and do something about this terrible addiction of mine. I will never stop thinking about Donald, he is part of me and he is there every day of my life. Although I wish every day that I didn't have to give him up, I will never try to interfere or demand anything from you. You are Donald's parents now and that is how I will think of you from now on. The thought of that makes me feel happy and removes so much of the sadness of giving Donald up.

I have said goodbye to Donald. I kissed him and touched him one last time. He seems so happy, full of life. I look forward to hearing about all the amazing things you will do with him and the wonderful life he will be leading.

Needless to say, we were in bits by the time we finished the letter. We were sad for Michelle but at the same time we knew we were so lucky. We had found a child to love, to call our own, we would know what it means to be parents and we would try to make Michelle a part of this family, too.

Epilogue
LOVE WORKS

People who have suffered from a lack of love are driven to find a substitute because one cannot survive as a human without receiving and giving love. Being shown love through touch, through cuddles, is incredibly important to us, so much so that many people damaged through lack of love as children use sex as a way to 'feel' love, and to feel as though they are wanted and that it is possible for them to be loved. Addictions and this kind of sex are poor substitutes for love, though – the drugs really don't work. The brain, 'fooled' by its orbital frontal cortex into placing fake desires above genuine needs, is never satisfied with what it receives in place of love. It cannot relax and let its 'owner' get on with life.

And when these love-starved people become parents, the cycle is perpetuated. They fail to attune with their children because, as long as they continue to feed their addiction, until someone shows them how to love, they don't know how. They are unable to be emotionally present in a way that their baby will understand – the language of true love will be missing. This is an extremely subtle process which is easily undermined by brain processes damaged when the parent was a child. The parent might be fully attached to their child but not attuned – distracted by their addiction for example – and the child will sense this, becoming stressed, increasing their own chance of addiction in the future.

We shouldn't blame the parents. To paraphrase Philip Larkin's poem your Mum and Dad fuck you up, but they, in turn, were fucked up. The adopters who have spoken frankly for this book have shown one way that the cycle can be broken. As hard as the option of adoption is for all concerned, it is sometimes totally the right thing for child and parent; making the child safe and providing a way for the parent to heal.

Another way to break the cycle is through talking. Talking about the past to professional therapists – as well as to people who have lived through similar experiences. This changes the way a person thinks, and this changes brain chemistry. Their brains may have never had a chance in childhood but we have a chance to heal throughout our lives.

Finally, we shouldn't automatically despise drug addicts. It's hard not to because they are not pleasant to deal with. They're not good with reasoned argument (they might nod along and agree, and then do what they wanted anyway) and their brains are hardwired with the expectation that they will be treated harshly by anyone in authority. They tend to show hostility to those with power over them. They are confused by the drugs, consuming cocaine for the emptiness and heroin for the pain. But, behind all that, they are human, and they were children who needed help and didn't get it.

And – as I've said before – as adults, they need our love more than ever.

Sharon is one of the most important people in my life. I first met Sharon when she was a trainee social worker briefly assigned to me when I was coming up to eighteen years old. We became friends and we stayed in touch via the phone and the occasional visit for much of my adult life. Even when I was 'on the run' I still checked in with Sharon when I needed to hear a friendly voice, although I hid the turmoil I was going through from her. During the writing of this book we met up to talk about our relationship and I wanted to include a short piece of the transcript here because I think it really hits the nail on the head about the importance of having someone to talk to. Without her, I might not have made it. And Sharon's still helping me today, more than twenty years later.

Sharon: When I first met you, I was amazed at how bright, bubbly and perceptive you were. You were ballsy, asking lots of questions, you even asked for a picture of me. My first thought was: 'What's this young person on?' I felt a real connection with you. Parts of you reminded me of me, and there was something in you that made me wish I could be like that. You'd just ask questions and questions and questions. There was something in you that made me trust you, it was like an automatic instinct.

When you were pregnant and said you were getting

married, I felt a bit disappointed that you were going to do that. This wasn't a feeling that was related to the way I saw you professionally, as a social worker, I thought you were brighter than I was in school and hoped you'd become a solicitor. I really didn't understand why you were getting married. My first thought about the foster placement was that something wasn't right about it. Certain things stick with me, like that the foster carer was not someone I ever felt an affinity with and you were telling me little bits but seemed to be fine. And then when you left the foster home and made this big allegation . . . I'd only ever been in one room and hadn't seen the rest of the house. This woman had managed to hide things. If I had thought that something was really wrong I would have done something about it.

Hope: I decided not to go back into foster care and contacted social services. When they refused to do anything more for me because I was nearly eighteen, and I refused point-blank to accept that, they gave me one more placement with another foster carer but I could only stay until my eighteenth birthday. That's when I decided to get pregnant. That was the only reason I got pregnant, because they were throwing me out of care.

Sharon: As your social worker and now, over years of knowing you, my perception at the time was that you told me what you wanted me to know. I might have had a feeling – deep down – about you, but I didn't know what you were going through. I never knew things were drastically wrong with you; you have a way of making yourself look happy when inside you're feeling awful. I saw you as a resilient person but I didn't understand your decisions. I never realised you got pregnant so you wouldn't get kicked out of care. It's a social worker's responsibility to drag those things out of you and I feel bad about that now.

When you had both your children, that's when I knew you weren't really coping and then we had a lot of telephone conversations through the years. I thought you had support. You said you asked for support and then I made sure that someone was coming to see you.

When you asked me when I was going to see you, I felt a responsibility to come. I wanted to see you in your house but I felt there wasn't much I could do. You were telling me things but not the most important things – that you were still this little girl who walked into the police station asking for help all those years ago. In fact, we had a laugh when I visited, you were a ball of sunshine, bursting with energy, although you did say you thought you needed to be a young person, but had found yourself in an adult role as a mother. I know you needed to be out there being young. What I didn't know was how important I was to you. I thought it was important we spoke, but I never analysed it. From what you told me, I thought you had a certain level of support and I thought that was enough, but I suppose I questioned myself over the years – whether it was right for me to be in a friendship with you. You were resilient but I could see your vulnerability.

Hope: What kept me resilient was the love and care of other people in my life. I got angry with them when I felt they were making the wrong decisions; they weren't horrible people. I needed and wanted people in my life and the love outweighed all of the strife. You gave me so much. Do you think I broke professional boundaries?

Sharon: We'd already gone past that. It was no longer to do with social work. It just happens that we met each other through social work. That's why I didn't feel too overwhelmed because I had made that choice. I had a good feeling about you. You trust people first and then see if that trust is borne out through actions. Often it's the other way around. Both of us trusted our feelings.

Hope: When we first met, I thought you were so cool. I had gone from a 'typical' social worker – white, middle class, bead necklaces, glasses hanging around her neck and a leather satchel – to you. You were just a few years older than me and beautiful. I did see you as an authority figure but not in a scary or alienating way. I put on a mask and said I was going to get married when I had to leave care because I needed to show the world that I was a responsible woman. I've talked a lot in this book about love and a bit about the power of physical touch, but just having a social worker to stay in touch with on the phone can make all the difference. It did to me.

Sharon: That's true; it may be nothing more than being available on the other end of the phone and making sure the person has the contacts they need. While it helps if you can ring someone you know, even then you can only get a *sense* of how that person is. You'll never *really* know how they are feeling. You can be alone even if you have people around you. The actor Robin Williams once said that people think that being lonely is the worst thing ever. It's not; it's being with someone and being lonely. Your way of coping with that was drinking. I agree that touch is also very important. When I was living alone, a woman across the road there opened up a massage parlour and I used to go over there so I could have a massage. It's not just about releasing stressed muscles, it's the healing touch.

Hope: You can also touch somebody through tone and expression, even on the phone if your tone is right, if you can identify.

Sharon: If you had been a different person, then the contact we had might not have happened. But it felt good to me, because you had so much positive energy. It was very important for you to have contacts like me and I understood that, and there was no risk for me that I could see. There could have been if you'd become mentally ill and told people that we'd crossed professional boundaries. And if you said something that suggested you were going to hurt yourself or someone else, then I'd have had to ring social services. Each county needs a service that has support workers to help young people when they leave care. Incidents might still occur, but there'd be a lot less of them.

Hope: I didn't drink when I was pregnant with either of my babies. It wasn't out of concern for their health; I would love to say that. The midwife told me to drink some Guinness as that's supposed to be full of iron [this isn't true, it's got a microscopic amount of iron] and I couldn't keep it down. My body just rejected it. I always drank to get drunk. When I got my files and I was with Dan and had the children and my home, that was when it hit me really hard and I totally embraced alcohol to get through the emotions that came flooding back. I needed to blank it all out. That's when the alcoholism progressed. I was clinically depressed. The outreach worker would come around and the kids would let her in. I'd be lying on the sofa, not saying anything. She got me to the doctor. That is why I am so hot on what I need to do to stay in recovery. When depression strikes I withdraw and don't talk to people and I believe the thoughts that tell me I'm a piece of shit. So many people in recovery suffer from clinical depression. I believe I was born with the ability to bounce back, and I'm lucky that the people in my life have nurtured this ability to the point where I won't allow the depression to take over without doing something about it.

Sharon: There are days, aren't there? When we feel so alone, looking at a grey, sad world.

Hope: But as long as there's love . . .

ACKNOWLEDGEMENTS

First off, thank you to my beautiful agent, Rebecca Winfield; my goodness, girl, you've got your work cut out with me! I cannot fail to share my absolute gratitude to my loyal editor, Kerri Sharp, and publicists Helen and Sam, who, as always, have taken my disorganisation in their stride.

My thanks as always have to go to my family – I know you 'lose' me while I'm writing these books, but thank you so much for understanding why I feel compelled to deliver these stories.

Lastly, my thanks to all of the contributors who have so kindly agreed to share their stories. While I have changed details to protect them, the facts remain true.

I hope I have remained true to your histories as I promised I would.

Finally, for those interested in the psychology of addiction, *In the Realm of Hungry Ghosts* by Gabor Mate (M.D) (Random House Canada, 2013) is probably the definitive scientific account and was most helpful to me when writing the chapter entitled 'The Love Addiction'.